Edouard Naville, Thomas H. Lewis, Joseph J. Tylor, Francis L. Griffith

Ahnas el Medineh - Heracleopolis Magna

with chapters on Mendes, the nome of Thoth, and Leontopolis - Vol. 11

Edouard Naville, Thomas H. Lewis, Joseph J. Tylor, Francis L. Griffith

Ahnas el Medineh - Heracleopolis Magna
with chapters on Mendes, the nome of Thoth, and Leontopolis - Vol. 11

ISBN/EAN: 9783337288396

Printed in Europe, USA, Canada, Australia, Japan

Cover: Foto ©Andreas Hilbeck / pixelio.de

More available books at **www.hansebooks.com**

AHNAS EL MEDINEH
(HERACLEOPOLIS MAGNA)

WITH CHAPTERS ON MENDES, THE NOME OF THOTH, AND LEONTOPOLIS

BY

EDOUARD NAVILLE

AND APPENDIX ON BYZANTINE SCULPTURES

BY

PROFESSOR T. HAYTER LEWIS, F.S.A.

THE TOMB OF PAHERI
AT EL KAB

BY

J. J. TYLOR, F.S.A., AND F. LL. GRIFFITH, B.A., F.S.A.

ELEVENTH MEMOIR OF

THE EGYPT EXPLORATION FUND.

PUBLISHED BY ORDER OF THE COMMITTEE.

LONDON:
SOLD AT THE OFFICE OF THE EGYPT EXPLORATION FUND, 37, GREAT RUSSELL STREET, W.C.;
AND BY KEGAN PAUL, TRENCH, TRÜBNER & CO., PATERNOSTER HOUSE, CHARING CROSS ROAD;
B. QUARITCH, 15, PICCADILLY; A. ASHER & CO., 13, BEDFORD STREET, COVENT GARDEN.

1894

GENERAL VIEW OF THE TEMPLE OF HERACLEOPOLIS MAGNA.

AHNAS EL MEDINEH

(HERACLEOPOLIS MAGNA).

PREFACE.

The present memoir comprises the result of two campaigns; and it bears testimony to what every experienced excavator knows only too well, that sites which at first sight seem the most promising are often those which cause the greatest disappointment.

But still, although I did not find at Ahnas remains of the Xth and XIth dynasties, as I had hoped, and although Tmei el Amdid and Tell Mokdam yielded only a few monuments, the excavations at those places have by no means been barren. They have materially contributed to the solution of historical and geographical questions, and have thus furthered the progress of Egyptology. Besides, the Byzantine ornaments discovered at Ahnas are quite unique among the products of Christian art in Egypt.

I have particularly to thank my eminent friend, Prof. Erman, for the map of Ahnas, which he drew during his visit to the spot with Dr. Schweinfurth.

As in the former memoirs, the linear plates have been drawn by Mme. Naville, and the phototypes have been executed from negatives taken by the Rev. Wm. MacGregor and myself.

EDOUARD NAVILLE.

Malagny, *July*, 1893.

CONTENTS.

	PAGE
HERACLEOPOLIS MAGNA—	
Its Origin and its Name .	1
Divinities of Heracleopolis	7
Monuments Discovered	9
The Necropolis .	11
MENDES .	15
THE NOME OF THOTH	22
LEONTOPOLIS .	27
APPENDIX ON BYZANTINE SCULPTURES FOUND AT AHNAS	32
INDEXES	35

HERACLEOPOLIS MAGNA;

ITS ORIGIN AND ITS NAME.

About twelve miles north-west of the town of Beni Suef, the great canal which bounds the cultivated land, i.e. the Bahr Yusûf, makes a strong curve towards the east. There it skirts huge mounds of decayed houses, covered with masses of broken pottery, and a few granite monuments scattered here and there amongst them. The mounds extend over an area of 360 acres. They are popularly known as Omm el Kemân, the *Mother of Mounds*, because of their size. The Copts called the place *Ahnas*; its official name is Henassiet el Medineh, *the city of Henassieh*, and it has long been recognized as the site of Heracleopolis Magna.

The greater part of these mounds is waste land, utilized by the inhabitants for *sebakh* digging only. This is especially the case with the mound called *Kom el Dinâr*. But several hamlets and villages now occupy the site, the most important of them being the one called *Melaha*. Just in front of this village are four standing columns, called the *Kenisch*, or *church*, and belonging to a Roman or Byzantine edifice. Two abandoned saltpetre pits are also to be found. They were used at the beginning of this century in the manufacture of gunpowder for the Mamelukes and Mohammed Ali. Although this was the occasion of much digging, it does not seem to have led to the discovery of any antiquities. The place must have been important in the time of the Greek emperors, before the Mohammedan conquest, for it contains the ruins of several Coptic churches—chiefly bases and shafts of columns, some of them very large. But nothing indicated the site of an ancient Egyptian temple, and yet there had been more than one. It was by mere guess-work that we discovered the place where the god *Arsaphes* had his dwelling, and we made many soundings before we hit upon it in a depression west of the Kom el Dinâr. One may form an idea of the labour required for discovering and clearing the remains of this temple, when I say that, to this end, I was obliged to remove more than 40,000 cubic metres of earth. We do not know at what date Heracleopolis was founded, but very anciently it was one of the important cities of Egypt. Manetho says that the IXth and Xth Dynasties were Heracleopolitan, and, even from the scanty information which has come down to us, we must conclude that Heracleopolis played an important part in the events of that obscure period. The tombs of Sioot, attributed to the Xth Dynasty by M. Maspero and Mr. Griffith, describe the wars waged on behalf of their Heracleopolitan sovereign by the vassal princes of Sioot, probably against rebels from Thebes. Hence, there is frequent mention of the city of Heracleopolis in these inscriptions, and even the name of one of the kings who is supposed to have resided there is also given. We might therefore have reasonably expected that our excavations would throw some light on those dark times, and help us to fill up this great historical gap in our present knowledge. Mariette entertained great hopes as to excavations in the mounds of Ahnas. He reverts to the subject several times in his last memoir, published in 1870, and which has justly been called his Archaeological Will.[1] "C'est à Ahnas el Medineh, représentée aujourd'hui par des ruines assez étendues, qui n'ont été jusqu'ici l'objet d'aucune investigation sérieuse, que nous devrons essayer de faire revivre des souvenirs des IXe et X^e dynasties." But these hopes, in which I also shared, have been completely disappointed; the oldest remains which I found in the mounds of Ahnas belong to the XIIth Dynasty.

One of the most ancient references to the city of Heracleopolis exists in a tale, whose origin may be assigned to the XIIth or XIIIth Dynasty,[2] although the events which it relates are supposed to take place much earlier, under the reign of Nebkaru of the IIIrd Dynasty. It describes a quarrel between a peasant and a huntsman who had robbed him. The matter was referred to the head of the officials, *the high steward, Merutensu* 𓂝𓏤𓉐𓇓𓏏𓊪𓏤 at Heracleopolis, who declares himself that he will have to report the litigation to the king. If we could rely on the information derived from this tale, it would appear that at that remote epoch *Hunensu* was not yet a great city, but rather a village belonging to the royal domains, and where the highest authority was invested in the power of the steward or royal agent, the *Nazir* as we should say now. But we must not forget that this is a tale, a kind of romance, and not an historical document. Its description of the city in no way agrees with the eminence of Heracleopolis in mythology, a point which we shall have to consider later, nor yet with the oldest historical text wherein the city is mentioned, and which dates from the XIIth Dynasty.

The XIIth Dynasty, which, as we may judge from its important work in the Fayoom, had a special liking for this district, could not well neglect Ahnas, and we have proof that it did not, in a stele engraved on the rocks of Hamamât.[3] It belongs to an officer called 𓂝𓏤𓉐𓇓𓏏 *Khnui*, who relates that in the fourteenth year of his reign, 𓇋𓏏𓏤 𓏤 𓆄 𓃀 𓃀
𓏤𓉐𓊪𓂝𓇋𓂝𓉐𓉐𓂝𓏤𓊪𓏤𓂝𓉐𓏤𓏤
𓏤𓇋𓂝𓂝𓊪𓂝𓏤𓉐𓏤𓂝𓊪𓏤𓉐𓏤𓏤
His Majesty ordered him to go to Rohennu (Hamamât), in order to bring the fine monuments which his Majesty erected to Hershef (Arsaphes) the lord of Hunensuten. This inscription belongs to the reign of Usertesen III., but as the king erected statues at Hunensuten to the god of the locality, it is clear that the temple in which they were erected must have existed before them. In fact, the architraves raised by Rameses II., for the construction of the vestibule which he added to the temple, bear the standards of Usertesen II. I am therefore quite unable to share Professor Flinders Petrie's opinion,[4] when he says that the blocks with the name of Usertesen II. at Ahnas came from the temple of Illahun, which Rameses II. destroyed in order to build the temple of Heracleopolis. Whatever changes Rameses II. may have made in the sanctuary of Arsaphes, he was not its founder. It is even probable that for this event we must go much farther back than the XIIth Dynasty, for if Hunen-

---

[1] *Questions relatives aux nouvelles fouilles à faire en Égypte*, p. 25.
[2] Chabas, *Pap. de Berlin*, p. 5; Id., *Mélanges*, p. 249; Maspero, *Contes*, p. 35.
[3] Lepsius, *Denk.*, ii. 136, a.
[4] *Kahun, Gurob and Hawara*, p. 22.

suten was the capital under the IXth and Xth Dynasties, how can we picture to ourselves an Egyptian city without its temple, the nucleus of its foundation, the central point around which the inhabitants gathered and built?

The name of Heracleopolis Magna is in Egyptian [hieroglyphs] or [hieroglyphs] with a great number of graphic variants. Several readings have been proposed for the name; they differ chiefly in the value given to the sign [glyph] which is polyphonous, and which in many instances is to be read $\circ$ *Khen*.[5] The correct reading seems to me to have been determined by Professor Brugsch,[6] who quotes a variant found in a papyrus of the XVIIIth Dynasty,[7] where the name is written [hieroglyphs].[8] Admitting that the two signs [glyph] [glyph] have been inverted, and should be written [glyph] [glyph], the reading of the whole name would be *Hunensuten*, or abridged, *Hunensu*, whence we can easily trace the origin of the ⲉⲛⲏⲥ of the Copts, and the اهناس of the Arabs.

Are we to recognize in this name the city of חָנֵס which is mentioned once in Scripture by the prophet Isaiah (xxx. 4)? In opposition to the view of the majority of commentators, I believe with Professor Brugsch and Professor Duemichen that the city of *Hanes* mentioned by Isaiah is to be looked for in the Delta. Let us look at the context, at the circumstances which induced the prophet to speak of Hanes, and at the passage itself as given in the Revised Version.

"The plan which the Jews had hidden from the prophet (xxix. 15) had been matured, and ambassadors had been sent to Egypt with rich presents. Isaiah makes of this accomplished fact a ground for denouncing the alliance concluded in enmity to God, and which will only avail to put the Jews to shame."[9] "Therefore," says the prophet, "shall the strength of Pharaoh be your shame, and the trust in the shadow of Egypt your confusion; for his princes are at Zoan, and his ambassadors are come to Hanes." The sense seems to be very clear. Pharaoh is willing to side with the Israelites, he will not turn his back against them, on the contrary, he will receive them with every sign of goodwill. His princes, the chief of his troops are in Tanis, not very far from the eastern frontier, and his ambassadors are even farther, waiting for the arrival of the Israelites who come to beg for his support. It seems difficult not to understand the word *ambassadors* as referring to men sent forward to meet the Israelites, and in that case they must be the vanguard of the king and of his army. If his princes are in Tanis, his ambassadors cannot be a long way behind; they must be in advance, at the eastern border of the country. Thus we are compelled either to admit the reading of the Chaldaean version תְּחַפְנְחֵס *Daphnae*, the eastern bulwark of Tanis, or to suppose that there was in the Delta a city called *Hanes*. This latter alternative seems to me the more probable. If we turn to the great inscription of Assurbanipal, in which the Assyrian king relates his wars against Tahraka, or as he calls him Tarqû, we find that among the cities to which his father had appointed governors there is one called *Khininsi*. Here again Oppert[1] and other Assyrian scholars have admitted that the name referred to Heracleopolis. But as it occurs among the names of cities which all belong to the Delta, immediately after Athribis and before Sebennytos, Mendes,

---

[5] Duemichen, *Geogr. Inschr.*, Text, ii. p. 20.
[6] *Zeitschr.*, 1883, p. 76.
[7] Naville, *Todt.*, ii. pl. 293, Pt.
[8] In the name [glyph], Duemichen, *Geogr. Inschr.*, ii. pl. xxxvi. 13, the sign [glyph] has the value [glyph].

[9] Dillmann, *Jesaia*, p. 268.
[1] *Mém. sur les rapports de l'Égypte et de l'Assyrie*, p. 91; Haupt, *Zeitschr.*, 1883, p. 86.

and Busiris, it would be extraordinary if it applied to a city of Upper Egypt. Therefore we must conclude that there was a Khininsi in the Delta, for which the hieroglyphic equivalent would be ⸺ *Khens*, which Professor Duemichen considers as being the hieroglyphic name of Daphnae. Whether we admit his conclusion or not, we must give up the idea that Heracleopolis is mentioned in Isaiah. Heracleopolis is not named in the Bible. Hanes is not the capital of the XXth nome of Upper Egypt, it is more north, on the frontier of the country. As for the name Hanes, it is probably the same as 'Ανῦσις, which is found in Herodotus.² The Greek author mentions it twice, once as being the birthplace of the king of the same name, and again as being one of the cities of the Calasirians, all of which, except Thebes, are cities of the Delta.

It is very difficult to determine the exact boundaries of the Heracleopolitan nome. The two authorities on which we must chiefly rely, Strabo and Ptolemy, agree in stating that the nome lay in a great island. Ptolemy gives us the latitudes of the two points where the Nile divided itself into two branches, and where the branches reunited. According to him, the river divided itself at latitude 29° 30′, and the two branches met together at latitude 28° 45′.³ In fact, we must reverse the expressions used by the Egyptian geographer, who describes the nomes from north to south like a traveller going up the Nile.⁴ What seems to him the point where the two branches separate is, on the contrary, the place where they again unite, while farther south, the place where the branches are said to meet together is really the point of their separation. According to Ptolemy, the island had a length of three-quarters of a degree. It contained two important cities, Heracleopolis, situate on the western branch of the river which embraced the island, and Nilopolis,⁵ quite inland.

Strabo,⁶ in a somewhat obscure passage, says that near the island on the right was a canal running towards Libya and the Arsinoite nome. It had two openings and cut the island in two. The French archæologist Jomard,⁷ who must be credited with the discovery of the site of Heracleopolis and the identification of the city, considers that the canal described by Strabo is the same as the western branch of the Nile mentioned by Ptolemy, consequently he gives the following boundaries: on the east, the Nile; on the west, the Bahr Yusûf; on the north and on the south, two transversal canals cut across the valley. He gives the starting-point of both of them; for the southern, at a place called *Harabchent*, and for the northern, at *Zawch*, near the present railway station of *Wasta*.

Jomard's argument seems to me to be based on an erroneous interpretation of Strabo. It is impossible to suppose that the canal mentioned by the Greek geographer skirted and limited the island on the west, since Strabo says that it cut through the island, and separated part of it from the rest. Moreover, for Strabo, an island is not artificial, not a piece of land en-

---

² Her., ii. 137, 166.
³ Ed. Bertius, p. 126.
⁴ εἶτα καθ᾿ ὅ μέρος σχίζεται ὁ ποταμὸς ποιῶν νῆσον τὸν Ἡρακλεοπολίτην νομὸν καὶ ἐν τῇ νήσῳ Νείλου πόλις μεσόγειος—καὶ μητρόπολις πρὸς τῷ δυτικωτέρῳ τμήματι τοῦ ποταμοῦ Ἡρακλέους πόλις μεγάλη, καὶ ἐν τῇ νήσῳ Νείλου πόλις μεσόγειος (p. 125).

⁵ I consider that the site of Nilopolis is that of the place now called Aboosir.
⁶ ......πλὴν εἴ πού τις ἐντρέχει νῆσος, ὧν ἀξιολογωτάτη ἡ τὸν Ἡρακλεωτικὸν νομὸν περιέχουσα (p. 789).
εἴθ᾿ ὁ Ἡρακλεώτης νομὸς ἐν νήσῳ μεγάλῃ καθ᾿ ἣν ἡ διῶρυξ ἐστιν ἐν δεξιᾷ εἰς τὴν Λιβύην ἐπὶ τὸν Ἀρσινοίτην νομόν, ὥστε καὶ δίστομον εἶναι τὴν διώρυγα μεταξὺ μέρους τινὸς τῆς νήσου παρεμπίπτοντος (p. 809).
Μετὰ δὲ τὸν Ἀρσινοίτην καὶ τὸν Ἡρακλεωτικὸν νομὸν Ἡρακλέους πόλις ἐν ᾗ ὁ ἰχνεύμων τιμᾶται ὑπεναντίως τοῖς Ἀρσινοίταις (p. 812).
⁷ *Descr. de l'Égypte*, *Antiquités*, vol. iv., p. 401, ed. Panckoucke.

circled by canals; for him an island must owe its existence to the Nile itself, it must be natural, and due to a division in the bed of the river itself. We must therefore admit that, in the times of Ptolemy and Strabo, the Nile divided into two branches somewhere between the present stations of Beni Suef and Feshn. We cannot consider the description of the two writers as referring to an island produced by canals; it was a more important stream, part of the river itself, which formed it. The island was natural and not made by the hand of man. There are several such islands at the present day. The island of Heracleopolis was much larger, but similar to that which is now in front of the village of Luxor. Traces of a branch of the Nile are said to exist in the valley between Beni Suef and the valley; but we do not know when water ceased to flow into it. Variations in the course of the river must have occurred frequently, as they do to this day. Branches of the Nile are separated from the main river, and thus islands are formed which do not necessarily last for ever. For instance, the island of Thebes has changed considerably from what it was at the beginning of this century. The map of the French *savants* indicates that in their time by far the most important branch was the western. Now, on the contrary, the great mass of water flows in the eastern branch along the village of Luxor, whereas after the beginning of March it is quite easy to wade across the western river.

The island of Heracleopolis was formed by a division in the river itself, and the city was built on the western stream. That branch was not the present Bahr Yusûf. When it reached the desert of *Ssedment*, it may have followed what has since become the bed of the Bahr Yusûf in its lower course; but it is evident from Strabo and Ptolemy that, in their time, the important canal known as the Bahr Yusûf did not flow as it does now. If, as is probably the case, its bed is natural and not the work of man, a great part of it would have been silted up in the time of these Greek writers, and according to an Arab tradition it was reopened by the famous Sultan Saladin, who then gave it his name of Yusûf. Ptolemy gives us a convincing proof of the truth of this statement.* Speaking of the nome contiguous to that of Heracleopolis on the south, the Oxyrynchos nome, he says that its metropolis was inland, μεσόγειος. But the ruins of the city of Oxyrynchos, now called Behnesa, are on the bank of the Bahr Yusûf, exactly like those of Heracleopolis, which are described by Ptolemy as being on the western branch of the Nile. Heracleopolis was situate on an important stream of water which did not exist at Oxyrynchos, said to be μεσόγειος. Yet if the Bahr Yusûf had then followed its present course, the two cities would have been in absolutely similar situations, and there would have been no reason for saying that one was inland, and the other built on a river. We are thus led to the conclusion that, according to the Greek writers, the Bahr Yusûf in its present course cannot be very old. It is probably a work of nature enlarged and regulated by the hand of man. Possibly the kings of the XIIth Dynasty may have begun this system of regulation in connection with the works of Lake Mœris, which is always attributed to them. But certainly in the time of Ptolemy, the Bahr Yusûf was not the large stream which it is now, or the geographer would not have described the sites of Heracleopolis and of Oxyrynchos as being so essentially different.

Let us now turn to the hieroglyphic inscriptions, and see what information they afford as to the geography of the nome. If we consult a certain monument in the museum of Marseilles,º dating from the XIIIth Dynasty, we find what I believe to be one of the oldest names, if not

---

* Συνάπτει δὲ ἀπὸ μὲν δυσμῶν τοῦ ποταμοῦ νομὸς Ὀξυρυγχίτης, καὶ μεσόγειος μητρόπολις Ὀξύρυγχος (p. 126).
º *Recueil des travaux*, vol. i. p. 107 and ff.

of the whole nome, yet at least of the region around Heracleopolis. The officer for whom the statuette in Marseilles was sculptured was [hieroglyphs], *the follower of the King in the inner islands of Tesh.* Tesh I consider with Brugsch as meaning the region of the lake—*das Seeland*.[1] The sign ⌒ reads [hieroglyphs] and has as variant [hieroglyphs], and this leads us to an inscription of a much later epoch, in which are related the high deeds of Horus in his fabled wars against Set. When going down the river, the god reaches the neighbourhood of Heracleopolis, we read this:[2]

[hieroglyphs]

He showed his bravery at Seab, protecting Osiris of Anrudef, in Mesen of the right and Mesen of the left, which are the abodes of His Majesty in the inner islands. We have a detailed description of several parts of the nome in the texts[3] which relate the various episodes of the famous war. We there see that the locality called in the later text [hieroglyphs], Anrudef, was a great sanctuary of Osiris, and that part of the temple called [hieroglyphs] *the eastern abode,* or [hieroglyphs] *the good abode,* was dedicated to Isis, who was considered as protecting Osiris by her enchantments. The goddess kept watch over the god for fear that enemies might come by night from the western desert, called [hieroglyphs] *the desert* or *the mountain of Mer.* The eastern abode looked towards the south; it was to the south-west of the shrine of Osiris, and near to it. This shrine of Osiris *Hershef*, Arsaphes, is frequently mentioned in mythological and religious inscriptions; it is called [hieroglyphs] *Nar*, from the name of a tree which Brugsch considers as being a kind of acacia, and M. Loret as the oleander.

Heracleopolis is mentioned in several texts as being in the neighbourhood of Lake Moeris. We read also of a canal or a river, called [hieroglyphs] *hun*, from which the great basin derived its water. In this canal or river there was an opening [hieroglyphs], which may have been the lock through which the lake was filled, or the mouth whereby the canal emptied itself into the lake. Near this opening was the [hieroglyphs] *the beginning of the lake*, as we learn from the inscription of Piankhi.[4] Comparing the hieroglyphic data with what we read in Ptolemy, I am inclined to think that the canal or river called [hieroglyphs] is nothing but the western arm of the Nile, which, branching off near Beni Suef, formed the island of Heracleopolis. From this [hieroglyphs], either at Illahun or at Hawara, issued a canal which flowed into the lake, and which must have conducted a considerable volume of water in order to fill such an extensive basin. The filling of it could take place only when the inundation reached a certain height, as we learn from the Fayoom papyrus.[5] Though it is clad in a mythological garment, we need not despise the information given by that document, which says that when the rising Nile, called Ra, first showed himself at the column of Heracleopolis, which was used as a Nilometer, it took the god forty-two days to reach the lake, where he arrived on the 23rd day of the month of Thoth. This seems to indicate that Lake Moeris could only be filled after a considerable rise of the river.

---

[1] *Zeitschr.*, 1872, p. 89.
[2] Duemichen, *Temp. Inschr.*, i., pl. cii. 22.
[3] Naville, *Mythe d'Horus*, pl. xvii.

[4] Line 76.
[5] Brugsch, *Reise nach der grossen Oase*, p. 36 and ff.

DIVINITIES OF HERACLEOPOLIS.

THE tutelary divinity of Heracleopolis, to whom the great temple of the city was dedicated, was a peculiar form of Osiris called 𓈖𓍿𓆑, *Hershef*. The Greeks have transcribed it Ἁρσαφής, a name which, according to Plutarch, means "bravery."[a] His interpretation is correct, since one syllable of the word is the root 𓍿𓆑, which means courage, bravery, gallantry. It is natural, therefore, that the Greeks, who, as we may judge from Herodotus, were fond of giving Greek names to the Egyptian gods, should have assimilated Hershef to Heracles, and have called the city of Hershef, Heracleopolis. Hershef, like the god *Khnum*, to whom he has much similarity, is represented with a ram's head bearing the head-dress of Osiris. In the few representations which have been found in the temple, he takes the form of Osiris, who usually has a human head; of Harmakhis, with a hawk's head bearing the solar disk; of *Horus neb ma kheru*, Horus the justified, or rather the victorious lord, having a hawk's head with the double diadem; and also of Tum. All these forms were known excepting 𓍿𓆑, Horus the justified or victorious lord, which, to my knowledge, is a new form of the divinity.

A variant of the name of Hershef gives it quite a different meaning. In a text of the XIIth dynasty it is written 𓈖𓍿𓆑 *he who is on or near his lake*.[r] This shows the connection of the god of Heracleopolis with Lake Mœris, and it is remarkable that this spelling should be found in a text belonging to the dynasty which is said to have first dug the lake or used it for regulating the inundation.

Another reading is 𓈖𓍿𓆑 or 𓈖𓍿𓆑 *he who is on his sand*. It is found in the Book of the Dead.[s] This leads us to mythological legends referring to the god. "He who is on his sand," means the dead Osiris who has been killed by Set. The god has been mummified, his body is in a coffin, deposited, as usual, in a sandhill." This reading is used in hymns in which Thoth, or rather the deceased who speaks like the god, addresses Osiris, and restores him to life by his great power.[1] The Hermopolite nome, the nome of Thoth, was only a short distance from Heracleopolis.

One of the most common epithets applied to the god, and that from which the name of his shrine is derived, is written in various ways. It is written thus 𓈖𓍿𓆑 in the texts of the XIth Dynasty,[2] and 𓈖𓍿𓆑 in the temple (pl. i. e.). This latter is found as late as the Saitic epoch.[3] Both these forms must be read *anauref*. In the later texts it is written 𓈖𓍿𓆑 *aurudef*. This name of the god or of the shrine is very often met with in Egyptian mythology, and the god to whom it applies is either a man standing, wearing the *Atef* head-dress, and holding a sceptre (pl. ii. c.), or, more properly, Osiris in the form of a mummy, having in his hands the emblems of judgment.[5] It is in connection with this name that the Egyptians give us a specimen of the etymology, or rather of the pun from which this name was derived: 𓈖𓍿𓆑 *none of his enemies bind him in his name of Anauref*,

---

[a] δηλοῦντος τὸ ἀνδρεῖον τοῦ ὀνόματος. Plut., *De Is. et Os.*, ch. 37.
[r] Lepsius, *Denkm.* ii. 136, a.

[s] 141, 76; 183, 1.
[1] *Todt.*, c. 182, 183.
[2] Pierret, *Mon. du Louvre*, i., pl. 17.
[3] Naville, *Mythe d'Horus*, pl. xv. et xvi.
[4] Naville, *Mythe d'Horus*, pl. xvi.
[5] Mariette, *Mon.*, pl. 21.
[u] *Todt.*, vign. to chap i.
[v] Lepsius, *Aelt. Denk.*, pl. 32

the pun being in the word [hieroglyphs], which means "to bind,"⁷ or perhaps also "to oppress."
The sanctuary of Heracleopolis is very often referred to in the Book of the Dead. It is spelt in the older texts [hieroglyphs], [hieroglyphs], *annaref*, or *annaaref*, and once only [hieroglyphs], which is very nearly the reading of the texts of later date, [hieroglyphs] *anrudef.*⁸ Several cosmogonic and mythological events were supposed to have occurred at Heracleopolis or in its temple. According to the Book of the Dead, it was there that the coronation of Osiris and of his son took place. It is said⁹ that the royal crown was given to Osiris on the day when he was ordained to the leadership of the gods, which is the day *when the two earths were joined*. Horus also was ordained to succeed his father on the day of the burial of Osiris, *the beneficent soul which resides in Hunensuten*.¹ The expression—*the two earths were joined*, [hieroglyphs], which is commented upon by this stronger word [hieroglyphs] *the two earths were united so as to make a whole*, seems to me to imply an allusion to an event which many late texts also locate at Heracleopolis, that raising of the firmament which caused the earth to become solid.² This seems to me the explanation of another sentence which occurs farther on in the same chapter of the Book of the Dead,³

[hieroglyphs] *Shu has beaten the two earths in Hunensuten*. The word used for beating, [hieroglyphs], which has been translated "pulverise, to grind to powder,"⁴ seems to me much rather to mean to beat in order to make more solid, to pound the earth either with an instrument or with the feet, so that it may become harder. This seems quite consistent with what we know of Shu, the uplifter of the firmament, who is seen standing with his feet on the earth, and lifting the sky with his arms. Although it was at Heracleopolis that the solidification of the earth took place, the god of the city was not merely a terrestrial god, he also became one of the inhabitants of the sky which had been raised on the spot where he was specially worshipped. In a hymn to Osiris Hershef, it is said that *Tonen places him in the firmament, in order that he may raise water over the mountains, that he may cause to grow what comes forth on the mountains, and the crops which grow in the plain*.⁵

Heracleopolis appears in the famous inscription of the destruction of mankind. It was the starting-point of the goddess *Sekhet* when she went out to trample upon the blood of the rebels, after she had destroyed them by the command of Ra. In a chapter of the Book of the Dead⁶ which I found in a Leyden papyrus, and which is unfortunately in a very bad state of preservation, there are traces of a narrative having some likeness to that of the destruction of mankind. We read that there were great rejoicings in Hunensuten and Annaref when Horus inherited the throne of his father and became lord of the whole earth. Afterwards it is said⁷ that *Suti* (Set) arrived, *his head drooping, and he prostrated himself in seeing what Ra had done . . . falling from his nostril*.

---

⁷ Brugsch, *Dict. Suppl.*, p. 11.
⁸ Brugsch, *Dict. Geog.*, p. 346.
⁹ Chap. xvii. 83-86 of my edition. I quite agree with M. Maspero that the mention of Hunensuten in l. 4 is an interpolation.
¹ Throughout this passage, the text of the tomb of Horhotep, which has been used by Mr. Le Page Renouf in his admirable translation, is more corrupt than the papyri of a later date.
² Duemichen, *Geogr.*, p. 213 and ff.
³ Line 97.

⁴ Pichl, *Dict. pap. Harris*, p. 96.
⁵ Chap. 183, line 15.
⁶ Chap. 175.
⁷ Chap. 175, line 31.

Then Osiris covered with earth (lit. ploughed) the blood which came out of Hunensuten. The word *plough* is used here intentionally. It reminds us of the great festival which was celebrated at Hunensuten, the festival of ploughing: "*I take the hoe, on the day of the festival of ploughing*," says the deceased. This festival, in which Osiris was placed on his sledge, was also celebrated at Busiris, and there again there was a tradition of the companions of Set having been massacred and their blood covered with earth.[a]

The raising of the firmament was commemorated at Heracleopolis by a solemnity called *akh pet*. According to Brugsch,[b] it was celebrated on the first day of the month of Phamenoth, which in the Alexandrian calendar corresponds to the 25th of February.

The Book of the Dead gives us some supplementary information about the city, and about the divinities considered as inhabiting Hunensuten or Anaaref. Besides Osiris, there was *Shu* and *Beb* or *Baba*,[1] a typhonic god, who is called the oldest son of Osiris. We read also that there were two great ponds in which Ra, or the deceased, purified himself on the day of his birth. They are figured in the vignettes of Chap. xvii. The entrance through which the deceased went down into the lower world *Roset* was supposed to be the southern door of Anaaref, the sanctuary where Osiris was buried. In the middle of Anaaref was a pond of fire, over which a monster with a dog's head kept watch. At Hunensu, as at Heliopolis, there was a sacred phœnix.

An officer of the Saïtic period, called Hor,[2] recounts upon his stele the important repairs which he had caused to be made to the temple. He speaks of two vineyards which he had established there in order to provide wine for the god whom he called *Honeb*.[3] The Ptolemaic texts of Edfoo and Denderah give us further information about the worship which was celebrated in the city, and as to the traditions connected with the worship.

MONUMENTS DISCOVERED.

After long search and repeated soundings, we hit upon a capital with palm-leaves, in red granite, and we dug all round it to a depth varying from fifteen to twenty feet. We thus cleared what I believe to be all that is still extant of the great temple of Arsaphes. It is a rectangular hall, in the forepart of which is a row of six granite columns (see *Frontispiece*). The greater side had a length of more than sixty feet, and in the middle there was a door giving access to the temple itself. The row of columns was parallel to the longer side; the short one, where the colonnade ended, was only twenty-five feet long. This vestibule had a basement of very hard red stone, on which the walls were built in white limestone. A very few fragments of them have been preserved, but except those five or six blocks bearing traces of inscription, the whole of the walls have disappeared.

On both sides of the door, on the basement, the following inscription was engraved, with signs more than two feet high :—

The living Horus, the mighty bull who loves Ma, the lord of Sed periods like his father Phthah Tanen, the King of Upper and Lower Egypt, Usermara sotep en Ra, the son of Ra, the lord of diadems, Ramses, who loves Amen, erected these monuments to his father, Hershef, the lord of the two lands. At the

---

[a] Chap. 18, 25. [b] *Myth.*, p. 306.
[1] Pleyte, *Zeitschr.*, 1865, p. 54.
[2] Pierret, *Mon. du Louvre*, i., p. 14.

[3] Brugsch, *Dict. Suppl.*, p. 852.

end of the short sides, on the surface produced by the thickness of the wall, the name of Rameses II., "loving Hershef," is repeated. The god there bears his usual titles, ⌀, *the king of the two lands, the lord of the two territories;* of East and West, according to M. Maspero.⁴

On both sides of the door forming the entrance to the temple, there are two scenes, and in the middle of each is the cartouche of Rameses II. (pl. i. A, B). In one it is said of him that he loves Anauref, in the other the goddess Ma, the goddess of Truth and Justice. Above these cartouches is represented, on one side, Arsaphes giving the sign of life to the goose of the group ⌀ *the son of Ra.* On the other side, Harmakhis performs the same task. Below the scene is an inscription saying that the monuments of Rameses are *well established in the house of Arsaphes.* These last words induce me to think that the building to which this vestibule gave access was the chief temple of the city. It is clear that it was called *the house of Arsaphes*, ⌀. Now if we consult the great Harris papyrus,⁵ which recounts the donations made by the king Rameses III. to the various temples of Egypt, we find among them ⌀

⌀ *The slaves which he gave to the temple of Hershef, the King of the two lands,* 103. It seems to me quite evident that the royal grant was made, not to one of the places of worship of secondary importance, but to the chief temple of the city, to what we should call the cathedral; and therefore, considering that the temple to which this text refers is called by the same name as that we discovered, and that both in the papyrus and in the inscriptions Arsaphes bears the same

⁴ *Proc. of the Soc. of Bibl. Archæology,* xiii. p. 409.
⁵ Pl. 61, l. 13.

title, *King of the two lands,* we may legitimately infer that the edifice that we had so much difficulty in discovering was the great temple of Hunensu.

The colonnade which was on the western side of the vestibule consisted of six columns in red granite more than seventeen feet high, with palm-leaf capitals of very fine workmanship. Only one of them is perfect; it is now in the British Museum (pl. vi.). The shafts of these columns were covered with engravings of scenes of offerings to the local divinities. We have Hershef, the principal of the local gods, with a ram's head and wearing the so-called *Atef* crown; Osiris Anauref with a human head; Horus neb makheru, whom I believe to be the son of Osiris, who, according to the tradition recorded in the seventeenth chapter of the Book of the Dead, came to the throne on the day of his father's burial. To all these divinities Rameses II. offers frankincense, milk, wine, cakes. We have also Harmakhis *the great god,* and Tum *the lord of the two On,* a name which signifies the two parts of Egypt. In the blank space dividing these scenes of offerings, Merenphthah, the son of Rameses, has inscribed his name (pl. ii. D.).

Together with the columns, we found parts of the architraves which they supported (pl. v.). They had been re-used, for they were originally engraved with the name of Usertesen II. Part of the standard name of this king is still preserved (pl. i. D, E). We have already seen that there are historical records of the XIIth Dynasty having built at Heracleopolis, and I suppose that the reason why so little remains of the constructions of Usertesen is that he built in limestone. In several places we have proofs that the XIIth Dynasty built extensively in limestone, a material foredoomed to certain destruction. Granite only survives. Door-lintels, columns, or architraves, as in this case, have preserved the names of the original founders. It was so at

Khataaneh, where the whole temple has disappeared with the exception of a doorway bearing the name of Amenemha III. The Labyrinth is no more, because it was made of limestone; and so it has been with the great temple of Heracleopolis. Passing through the door of the vestibule we reach a hall with very large columns, of which only the bases remain. They are made of several pieces of limestone, and their diameter is over four feet. Exclusive of these few bases, of the vestibule basement, and of the columns—which owe their preservation to the hardness of their material—the great temple of Arsaphes has entirely disappeared.

In the vestibule were a few statues; some of them were hopelessly broken, or so much corroded by water that they had completely lost their original appearances and were altogether beyond recognition. A granite torso of natural size, without name, should I think be attributed to the XXth Dynasty, to one of the later Rameses (pl. x. c.). By far the best monument which we found, and nearly intact, is a sitting statue in hard limestone of Rameses II., of heroic size (pl. x. A, B). The colour of the monument was remarkably well preserved, and did not disappear after long exposure to the air. The whole body and the face is painted red, and the stripes of the head-dress are alternately blue and yellow, as it was in the case of the Rameses II. now at Geneva, when first I discovered it at Bubastis. Whether the colour was not so good in the one case as in the other, or whether it adhered less strongly to granite than to limestone, at any rate, it entirely vanished from the Rameses of Bubastis after a few days' exposure. On the sides of the throne are the usual titles of Rameses II.; in the inscription below he is said to be the worshipper of Arsaphes (pl. i. c.). This statue was broken in two, but could easily be mended. Except the beard and a piece of one of the elbows, there was nothing missing. It is of good XIXth Dynasty workmanship, and has been presented to the University of Pensylvania.

THE NECROPOLIS.

On the other side of the Bahr Yusûf, towards the south-west, there is a sandy and rocky ridge which separates Ahnas from the Fayoom, or from what was anciently Lake Moeris. This region is called Gebel Ssedment, from a village situate near the canal, and not far from which are the ruins of a Coptic convent. I am inclined to think, with Prof. Duemichen,[6] that the hieroglyphic name of that region was 𓉴𓉴𓈗𓈗𓈘𓈘 *Menment, the region of mounds or of mountains*, especially as the Fayoom papyrus[7] connects with that region two localities called 𓊪𓉴𓏤𓈅𓈅𓏥𓈙𓏪𓏌𓈅 *the place of sand north of the canal Hun*, of the canal which I consider as being the branch of the Nile which limited the island of Heracleopolis on the west, and 𓊪𓉴𓏤𓈅𓈙𓏌𓈅 *the place of sand south of the canal*.

The Gebel Ssedment, as its name indicates, is part of the desert, and absolutely barren, owing to its height over the valley of the Nile, which puts it out of reach of the water.

This Gebel Ssedment was the necropolis of the city, or at least part of it, for the number of the tombs there is altogether out of proportion with the population of so large a city, and it is quite possible that the main part of it is not yet discovered, and must be looked for farther west or south in the desert. Near the cultivated ground, in the lower part, are the tombs of the poorer classes. Above, cut in the rock, are those of the rich, which must have been luxurious, for even in ancient times they attracted the cupidity of robbers, were pillaged,

---

[6] *Geog.*, p. 227.   [7] Pl. i., ed. Pleyte.

and afterwards re-used for burials much more recent than the original ones.

The upper tombs generally consist of a vertical pit sunk to a depth which sometimes reaches twenty feet. They are quite plain, without any painting or sculpture; for they are cut in a calcareous rock so friable that to attempt any engraving or works of art upon its surface would have been futile. The pit opens out on either side into a chamber in which the dead were placed. There are sometimes as many as three chambers, all at the same height, and opening from three sides of the pit; but the usual number is two. The pits are filled with sand nearly to the top, and from their great number we might have hoped to find many interesting burials among them. But after having dug out one or two, we soon perceived that the whole necropolis had been re-used. The original owners of the tombs were gone, and so too were perhaps their first and second successors. They had been replaced by badly mummified bodies, generally resting on reed mats. As a rule, there were several bodies in one chamber, and the sand falling into the pit had heaped all the bones together into one corner. There were some few remains indicating what the original burials had been, and showing that the tombs were not intended for people of the lower classes, but for rich men and persons of high social standing. We found a great many small fragments of broken tablets of the XVIIIth and the XIXth Dynasties, some of them of good workmanship. There were also pieces of cloth carefully painted with scenes from the Book of the Dead. A few things had escaped the plunderers, but they were of no value. No doubt the robbers had left them because they did not find them worth the taking. We found, for instance, a considerable number of *usheblis* (funerary statuettes) of the coarsest description, made of wood, painted black, with the names painted on in yellow. Others were in red terracotta, and others again were merely pieces of wood to which the form of a mummy had been rudely given by means of a knife, while the name of the deceased was written with ink in hieratic. We found hundreds of these ugly objects, which I believe to be more ancient than the bodies which were afterwards placed in the tombs. They had not been worth stealing, and they fulfilled the same offices for the later occupants as for the first. We often found, in small niches on the right sides of the entrances to the chambers, little baskets containing the fruit of the dôm-palm, poppy-heads, and pieces of bread. Pigeon eggs were deposited in small holes in the walls. The baskets often contained also small implements, such as pins, combs, and kohl-cases. One of the tombs had been plundered imperfectly; there were no coffins, only bones lying on mats. But in the time of the XVIIIth Dynasty, which was also the time of the original owner, it must have belonged to a rich man, for in the sand we found a very fine *usheblti* made of stone, painted in black with a white enamel inscription in front. The name of the deceased was ⌧ *Osiris Hamenna*. On the right of the entrance to one of the chambers were two baskets, one of which contained two alabaster pots, a comb, a kohl-case, a pin, a small pot of black earthenware with a handle, and a fine perfume spoon, the handle of which represents a girl among reeds. The other basket also contained a black pot, a pin, a kohl-case, and another fine spoon, the handle of which consists of two *Bes* gods standing back to back. Beside this was a small square box, in which we found two blue porcelain rings—one of them bearing the name of Amenophis III., the other with an ⌧, the sacred eye,—a small blue frog, two small scarabs, an *uta* ⌧, and a little tablet with the name of *Menkheperra*, ⌧. Several of these little things were stolen, the box in which they were packed having been opened, partially rifled, and closed up again. However, the two spoons, the most valuable of all these small objects, have been preserved, and may be seen in the Egyptian Museum at University College, London.

In the lower part of the Necropolis the pits are much smaller, and contained little more than an unornamented rectangular box. Near the box were placed vases of coarse red pottery and sometimes small wooden figures, which seem to have belonged to a boat and its crew; also plain wooden head-rests, and a hoe —the wooden instrument called ▷ *mer*, which was used for tilling the land.

The first coffins we discovered were in large pits where a great many bodies had been thrown in without any order, and apparently with a neglect little in accordance with the feeling of respect which the Egyptians are supposed to have testified towards their dead. Some of them were hardly mummified, wrapped in mats, or in a bundle of palm sticks. Here and there appeared a coffin painted in brilliant colours, and with all the characteristics of a late epoch. The greatest number we discovered were on the top of a hill and quite at the surface. A rudimentary niche had been cut in the rock, and the coffin was covered with rubbish. Some of those coffins were typically very ugly (pl. xi. A.). Most of them contained the bodies of women, and the mummies were wrapped in much cloth, without any amulets. Some of them had the single ornament of a necklace of small shells and blue beads, from which hung a porcelain image of Bastit. There were no inscriptions giving the names and titles of the deceased. The best mummies found were in the large pits. Some of them were in three cases, the inner ones being of cartonnage, adorned with figures of divinities and scenes from the Book of the Dead (pls. vii., viii.). The two cases enclosing the cartonnage were painted in red. Several specimens have been brought to European museums. On these coffins we see the hands of the deceased crossed on the breast, and wearing as it were gloves made of net-work (pls. vii., viii.). In two of them the right hand lay by the side, while the left was crossed on the breast (pl. xi. c.). Though the name does not appear on these coffins, there are inscriptions referring to the scenes from the Book of the Dead painted upon them, and also this formula, which is exactly repeated on several of the wooden sarcophagi:

A royal offering to Osiris who resides in the Ament; he gives that thy ghost may appear and smell the flowers in the days of the festivals of Sokaris. He gives water to thy ghost, flowers to thy body, garments to thy mummy, thou art justified, Osiris for eternity.

It is evident that the Necropolis was used in later times. A proof of this remains in fragments of Greek tablets which we found in some of the tombs, and I believe most of the coffins must be assigned to Ptolemaic or Roman times. There are a few, however, to which a much earlier date may be assigned, and which, though they contained bodies contemporary with the Christian era, are yet the remains of an earlier, and perhaps of the original Necropolis. I should mention a plain rectangular yellow box, which was found empty and without its lid. It is exactly of the style of the XIth Dynasty. The inscription, written horizontally along the upper part, reads as follows :

A royal offering to Anubis on his mountains in the Necropolis, the lord of Teser (may he give) a good burial in the Kherneter to the beloved Hnat. Another coffin in sycamore wood, with the arms in very low relief and crossed on the breast, is of much later epoch (pl. xi. B). On the side are painted two Anubis, a god with a human head, and other figures. The inscription is nearly destroyed; what remains of it reads thus : [hieroglyphs] in favour of Hotepka, the son of the priest, the scribe Rames. I should think that this coffin is later than the XXth Dynasty. Near it were two blue porcelain scarabs.

Thus it is clear that no definite period or epoch can be fixed for the Necropolis of Ssedment. We have here a cemetery which has been used and re-used during centuries, and where we may come across fragmentary remains ranging from the XIth Dynasty to the time of the Romans. The majority of those fragments, especially of the stelæ, points to the XVIIIth and XIXth Dynasties. It is probable that we must trace the origin of the greater part of the Necropolis to the time of the great prosperity and power of Egypt, to the age of the Thothmes, the Amenophis, and even of Rameses II.; however, parts of it must be much older, as we may conclude from the presence of the coffin of the woman Hunt. But even though we trace it as far back as the XIth Dynasty, there is nothing whatever which we can consider as belonging to the Old Empire.

I attribute to the XIXth Dynasty the only statue which I found at Ssedment (pl. xii. B.).

It is a broken granite group found in the rubbish thrown into one of the pits to fill it. It represented a standing priest and priestess. The figure of the priestess is nearly broken off. On the back were two scenes of offerings (pl. i. F.); the priest stood before Arsaphes of Hunensu, and the priestess *Hunuri* offered two sistrums to Hathor, the goddess of the city.

As for the pottery, some specimens of which have been put together on pl. ix., it is difficult to date it with exactness, considering that it comes from a necropolis which has been used at various epochs. However, it is to be noticed that with few exceptions the whole of it was found in the poorest tombs, and even in those bearing unmistakable indications of a very late date. We also found fragments of terra-cotta coffins; the headpiece of one of them is represented on the same plate as the pottery. All the vases belong to the roughest kind of Egyptian pottery. The bottle-shaped vases, which are sometimes considered as being the oldest Egyptian pottery, were found close to the cultivated land, in that part of the Necropolis which I described as being the poorest, where there are only rectangular boxes and imperfectly mummified bodies, without any ornament or amulet. Whoever has seen the Necropolis of Ssedment will have no hesitation in considering those bottle-shaped vases as the latest work discovered there, later than the pieces of Greek inscriptions found close by. Consequently they must belong to Roman times.

MENDES.

The two mounds situate near the present station of Simbillaouin, and separated by a small village, bear the collective name of *Tum el Amdid*. Nevertheless, these two mounds mark the sites of two different cities. The southern mound, distinguished by the more markedly Roman characteristics of appearance, was called *Temi*, تمي, in the Middle Ages, and is now called *Tell Ibn es Salâm*. It is the ruins of the ancient city of *Thmuis*. The northern mound has a decidedly Pharaonic character. It was known as *El Mondid*, المنديد, in the Middle Ages, afterwards as *Tell Roba*, and is the site of the ancient *Mendes*. These two important cities stood close to each other; and although they may have co-existed in the time of Herodotus, Mendes was the first, the oldest; it was the capital of the nome, and gave its name to the province. Later on, under the Romans, we find that Thmuis is pre-eminent, while Mendes has fallen into the shade.

In the first place, let us consider the information to be derived from classical sources with regard to these two cities. Herodotus[1] mentions the Mendesian mouth of the Nile as not originating at the apex of the Delta, but from the Sebennytic branch. He also speaks of the Mendesian nome, and of the local cult of the city, and says that this nome, together with several others in Lower Egypt, was allotted to those whom he calls the Calasirians, who constituted a division of the military caste.

Among the nomes belonging to this military caste, he also mentions that of Thmuis, Θμονίτης; but this is evidently a mistake, and the solitary mention of any such nome. In his enumeration, Herodotus has given us the same nome twice over under different names. Strabo[2] twice refers to the city and nome of Mendes as being in the vicinity of the city and nome of Leontopolis. Ptolemy, the geographer, gives us the position of the nome of Mendes, to which he assigns Thmuis as the capital.[3] Already in his time this last city had superseded the ancient capital; and, judging from the extent of its ruins, it must have been a city as large as Mendes. Thmuis is mentioned by Josephus[4] as one of the places where Titus encamped on his march against Palestine. The Roman general used the Mendesian branch of the Nile for the transport of his troops. Its navigation would seem to have afforded an easy access to the sea even for a large fleet, since it was at this mouth of the river that Nectanebo, the last native king of Egypt, fought his desperate battle against the Persian troops of Pharnabazus, under the command of the Athenian general Iphicrates. This battle sealed the fate of Egypt, for from that time onwards the prophecy of Ezekiel was fulfilled, and no native ruler evermore reigned in the land.

The prosperity of Thmuis is indicated by

---

[1] Lib. ii., 17, 42, 43, 166.

[2] P. 802, 812.

[3] Μενδήσιος νομός καὶ μητρόπολις Θμουίς. Ptol., p. 124.

[4] Ἀνάπλει διὰ τοῦ Νείλου κατὰ τὸν Μενδήσιον νόμον μέχρι πόλεως Θμούεως. *Bell. Jud.*, l. iv., chap. 42, ed. Froben.

Ammianus Marcellinus,[5] who says that it was one of the four great cities of Egypt, the other three being Athribis, Oxyrynchos, and Memphis. According to the Itinerary of Antoninus,[6] it was twenty-two miles distant from Tanis, and forty-four from Heracleopolis Parva, the present Kantarah on the Suez Canal. Thmuis became one of the episcopal seats of Egypt, and the names of two of its bishops have come down to us: that of Serapion, who wrote a biography of St. Macarius, and that of Phileas, who suffered martyrdom under Diocletian. Under Arab rule both mounds belonged to the province of Murtâhia.

I devoted the greatest part of my time to the Pharaonic mound of Mendes. The remains are so scanty that it is hardly possible, from the mere sight of them, to form an idea of what the old city must have been, and of the buildings which it contained. Rightly to judge of their size and importance we must go back to ancient descriptions of the place. An Arab geographer of the fifteenth century, Abul-'Abbâs Ahmed ben Ali el Calcaschandi, gives the following account of the ruins: "The temple of Tumei, in the province of Murtâhia, on the north towards the city of Tumei, is in ruins. The common people call it the Temple of 'Ad. Remains of its walls and of the roof, made of very large stones, have been preserved to the present day. Over the entrance is a piece of limestone and gypsum. In the interior there are large cisterns of hard stone and of a very extraordinary description." And further: "Tumei is a city in ruins, in the province of Murtâhia, with considerable remains. I saw there a hall with columns of hard stone made of one single piece of a height of about ten cubits, erected on a basement also of hard stone."[7]

We find that the place had altered considerably by the end of last century, at the time of the French expedition.[a] The French savants speak of it as being covered by a confused mass of broken pottery, granite blocks, and ruined brick walls. The only monument which they found complete was the monolithic shrine, still standing, and to which we shall refer later. Besides the shrine, there were blocks of black granite, which have since disappeared, as well as three falling buildings whose remains covered the soil. Also, at a short distance from the monolith, were twenty-eight large oval-shaped stones, hollowed as for watering troughs, or coffins; and Jomard, remembering the passage in Herodotus which says that Pan, called Mendes, was worshipped here under the form of a he-goat, suggests that these coffins may have been destined for the embalmed bodies of those sacred animals. They are evidently the " cisterns of extraordinary description " which so astonished the Arab traveller.

Another Frenchman, who visited the place about the same time, noticed that the ground had been dug over for the limestone with which the walls of the ancient buildings were made. He also observed that the pavement of the largest temple was of sandstone, and was covered with yellow and red fragments from Gebel Ahmar, the Red mountain near Cairo. Everywhere he found traces of fire, thick layers of charcoal and calcined matter, burnt bricks, and half-vitrified fragments, and as he had seen the same things on other mounds, he concluded that fire had been the chief agent in the destruction of this city. No doubt many of the old Egyptian cities owe their destruction to fire; but the most destructive of all fires is that of the kiln, which in modern times has reduced to lime the walls of

---

[5] L. xxii. 16.   [6] P. 153, ed. Wesseling.
[7] I am indebted to the kindness of Count d'Hulst for these curious quotations.

[a] *Descr. de l'Égypte. Ant.*, vol. ix, p. 369 and ff., ed. Panckoucke.

a great number of buildings, including the most valuable XIIth Dynasty temples of the Delta. The scanty remains which the French saw at the beginning of this century have for the most part long since disappeared, and except the monolithic shrine, some of the coffins, and a few stray blocks of hard stone which could not be used, nothing remains either above or below the soil of the extensive buildings of the city of Mendes.

When I settled there, at the beginning of January, 1892, the only things visible were

DRAWING FOUND IN LEPSIUS' PAPERS.

the monolithic shrine (see Vignette), a few blocks originally forming the basements of the walls, and the sarcophagi of the sacred rams within the enclosure wall on the north side, besides a very large coffin in black granite with a casing of limestone, which must have been for a high official or even for a king, and which had already been discovered and opened—when, we do not know. It bears no inscription.

The shrine is an enormous monolith of red granite; its height is more than twenty feet, and its width twelve. There is a low roof in the form of a pyramidion with a very obtuse angle. Its granite base rests upon a high limestone basement, which extended not only under the monument itself, but also underneath the hall which contained the shrine. The shrine was evidently destined to contain the sacred emblems, for it had a door, probably made of precious wood. The limestone basement was quarried out not long ago, and a quantity of lime has been made out of it for a pasha's farm; so that at present the solidity of the monolith is endangered by the deep holes around it, into which blocks of the pavement have fallen. This quarrying seems to have been stopped lately, owing to the energy of the Museum authorities, otherwise the shrine would certainly have fallen to pieces, and that the more easily since deep cracks on the sides show that the stone is broken.

One of the French explorers, Girard,[9] says that in his time there were traces of erased hieroglyphs on the sides of the shrine. They are no longer discernible. Burton,[1] who visited the place about the year 1825, and who made a drawing of the shrine, could decipher a few signs which were probably on the cornice of the monument. They form the coronation cartouche of King Amasis of the XXVIth Dynasty, who is said in the same inscription to be the worshipper of 𓊃𓈖𓏏𓀭 *the living soul of Shu*. In the course of the excavations which I made near the monolith, I found the same cartouche with the words (worshipper of) 𓊃𓈖𓏏𓀭 *the living soul of Seb*, on a granite block. I shall revert later to the worship of Mendes indicated by these words. Whether the shrine was reconstructed by the Saïtes, or whether those kings merely engraved an inscription upon it, one thing is certain: the

---

[9] *Descr. de l'Égypte, Ant.*, vol. ix. p. 375.
[1] *Excerpta hier.*, pl. xli.

temple itself is older than the XXVIth Dynasty; for among the stones which belonged to the basement, there are several bearing the name of Rameses II. and of his son Merenphthah. Two of them have been cut into water-basins, both have the name of Rameses II., but on one of them it is written with a variant. I here give the sentence in full:[2] 𓉐𓂋𓏏𓇯 ⸺ *As long as lasts the sky thy statues last, Usermara setep en Ra, son of Ra, Rameses, beloved of Amen, the divine chief of On;* &c., with the same cartouches, *As long as thou lastest Ra lasts in the sky, King Rameses, the divine chief of On.* This title of "divine chief of On," which Rameses II. assumes here, is very rarely met with in his cartouche. It was adopted by several of the later Rameses of the XXth Dynasty. The second stone, which is placed symmetrically to this, has the usual cartouches of Rameses II.

The dynasty which seems to have specially worked at Mendes is the XXVIth. We have already seen that the shrine bore the name of Amasis. That of one of his predecessors, Psammetichus II., is on a small fragment of the statue of a priest. To Apries also must be attributed a monument which we have published elsewhere,[3] and which is now exhibited in the Museum at Ghizeh. It was found in one of the trenches which I opened in front of the monolith, and is a statue representing a standing king, of natural size, and made from the red limestone of Gebel Ahmar. It was broken in two, the head being separated from the body; the feet are lost. The statue was never finished, it is unpolished, and the traces of the toothed hammer with which the surface was rounded off may still be seen upon it. I believe that it was originally intended to be the portrait of Apries, one of the kings of the XXVIth Dynasty. I came to this conclusion by means of a fragment of the same stone, coming probably from the same monument, and which was found close to the torso. This fragment bears the following inscription: . . . 𓊃𓌢𓏏𓆣 . . . This inscription is on the middle part of the base of a statue, and as it gives us the standard name of Apries, it is natural to conclude that the statue, which according to all probabilities stood upon that base, was the statue of Apries. But it has not preserved its original characteristics. The face has been remodelled; the traces of alterations subsequently made in the features are seen, not only in the way in which the features are cut, but also in the colour of the stone. The statue was turned into that of a Roman emperor, whose likeness was sufficiently well indicated for it to be still recognizable, since the sight of the characteristic wrinkles in the forehead enabled Mr. Murray and Mr. Grueber at once to identify this portrait as being that of Caracalla, whose reign was marked for Egypt by a terrible massacre in Alexandria.

Another monument of Apries, which evidently comes from the Tell, is to be seen in a mosque of the neighbouring village of Roba. It is a piece of limestone with both cartouches of the king well engraved. I did not succeed in my repeated attempts to purchase the stone and to have it taken out of the wall.

Towards the north-east of the monolith are small mounds which are evidently remains of old buildings. Digging in one of them, I found a very fine Hathor capital, which apparently surmounted a monolithic column in black granite, of which several fragments are left. This Hathor capital is very different from those I discovered at Bubastis.[4] Instead of a diadem of asps over the hair, it has a small shrine, out of which an asp projects, and the whole capital

---

[2] Mariette, *Mon.*, pl. iv.   [3] *Arch. Report*, p. 2.   [4] *Bubastis*, pl. ix.

is in the form of a sistrum, a musical instrument which was one of the emblems of the goddess Hathor. The hair is not so heavy as in the Ptolemaic capital of Behbeit el Hagar;[6] the face has the aquiline type of the Ramessides; I should therefore attribute it to the XIXth or XXth Dynasty. I should think that the building to which it belonged was connected with the cemetery of sacred rams; perhaps it was the hall with columns described by the Arab geographer, where he saw those "cisterns" of extraordinary shape.

Before my excavations, Brugsch-Bey had worked at Tmei el Amdid for the Boolak Museum. The most important result of his work is a Ptolemaic tablet,[6] which, like all documents of that kind, is most valuable, because it gives us a great deal of information about the names of the nome, its cities, its temples, and the worship which was carried on there. The nome of Mendes, the XVIth on the list, was ⌇, which Brugsch first read *Kha*, but which probably has to be read *Hamehi*;[7] and its capital was ⌇ ⌇ ⌇ *Pa ba neb dad*, which Brugsch long ago recognized as being the origin of the name of Mendes, the *Bindidi*[8] of the Assyrian inscriptions. It is not to be confounded with another city of very similar name, ⌇ ⌇ *Pa usar neb Dad*, which is the capital of the IXth nome, the present city of Aboosir, near Samanood.[9] Mendes was not exactly on the banks of that branch of the Nile to which it had given its name; the city was joined to the river by a canal ⌇ ⌇ *Aken*. Besides the holy ram, to which we shall presently return, the divinities were: the child Harpocrates, and a goddess —a woman wearing on her head the emblem of the nome. She is called ⌇ ⌇ *Hamehi, the sacred woman who resides in the abode of the ram*. The name of this divinity is preserved on a monument which I saw in the house of a Greek in a neighbouring village; it is the base of a kneeling statue erected for ⌇ ⌇ ⌇ *the attendant of the high priest of On* (Heliopolis), *Horuta, the son of the high priest of On, Haru*.[1] His mother is called ⌇ ⌇ *the priestess of Hamehi, Shephont*.

But the chief divinity, whose animal embodiment was kept and fed in the temple of Mendes, was the so-called sacred ram. I will continue to call it a ram in this paper, because that is the traditional name of the animal, although to my mind it is decidedly a misnomer. I believe that the sacred animal of Mendes, whose conventional form, I admit, is more like that of a ram than anything else, is meant to represent not a ram, but a he-goat. It is remarkable that all the Greek and Roman authors who speak of Mendes and of the animal worshipped there invariably call it a he-goat, τράγος, and not a ram, κριός. Herodotus, Strabo, Suidas, Nonnus, Plutarch, are unanimous on that point; they say that the Greek god Pan was called Mendes by the Egyptians, that it had the form of a he-goat, and that therefore, in the Egyptian language, that animal is called Mendes.[2] On the other hand, the same authors repeatedly mention the ram (κριός) as being the symbol of Amon, or as the Greeks call the god Ζεύς, Jupiter. "The Egyptians give their statues of

---

[5] *Descr. de l'Égypte, Ant.*, vol. v. pl. 30.
[6] *Zeitschr.*, 1871, p. 81; 1875, p. 33.
[7] J. de Rougé, *Géogr. de la Basse-Égypte*, p. 114.
[8] Oppert, *Rapports de l'Égypte et de l'Assyrie*, p. 92; Delitzsch, *Wo lag das Paradies?* p. 316.
[9] *The Mound of the Jew*, p. 27.

[1] See *Festival Hall of Bubastis*, pl. i. 4, the ⌇ ⌇ preceding the high-priest of On. Probably the son began with being the attendant of his father before himself attaining to the dignity of high-priest.
[2] Bochart, *Hierozoicon*, l. ii. p. 642; Jablonski, *Panth. Aeg.*, l. ii. cap. vii.

Jupiter the face of a ram," says Herodotus,³ and his statement is confirmed by several other authors and even by some of the Fathers. Lepsius⁴ has very clearly pointed out the distinction to be established between the ram-headed Amon and the other divinities, also called ram-headed, Khnum and Arsaphes. He has shown that Amon has horns going round the ear, and turning downwards, the regular ammonites or horns of Amon, while Khnum has always two horizontal horns diverging in a spiral line from a knot which projects out of the top of the head. Frequently also Khnum, like the sacred animal of Mendes, has four horns, those of Amon round the ear, and the upper horizontal ones. It is quite possible that this slight difference is meant to show in a conventional way that the animals were different; the horizontal, spiral horns pointing to the he-goat, while the horns of Amon indicate a ram. Let us remember that we are not to look for zoological accuracy in religious representations. There are certain laws, certain religious prescriptions which regulate the conventional forms of the sacred animals, and which absolutely prohibit others. Neither picture nor sculpture of a he-goat has ever been found in an Egyptian temple; we find only the so-called ram. Yet in spite of their never being represented, the testimony of classic writers is so clear and so positive, that it is quite impossible not to believe that there were sacred he-goats in Egypt as well as sacred rams, bulls, crocodiles, and cats. In the same way we never see swine, but always a hippopotamus, though we know that swine were sacrificed at certain festivals. It is quite possible that, by a similar conventionalism, the horned ram may be the religious form of two different animals, the two-horned one being the ram, and the four-horned the he-goat. Another proof, which seems to be very convincing, is afforded by the study of the coins.⁵ The coins of Thebes, or of Diospolis Parva in the Delta, all bear a ram drawn in the most distinct way, and not to be mistaken for any other animal; while the coins of Mendes bear a he-goat just as clearly and distinctly drawn as the ram of Thebes.

I cannot enter here into a full and exhaustive discussion of this subject, which requires attentive consideration. For the present I shall keep to the old name, given, as I believe, merely on account of the animal's appearance in the sculptures, and based on a wrong interpretation of a conventional form. I shall therefore continue to speak of the sacred ram of Mendes. I only wish to point out that the usual opinion as to the real nature of the animal does not seem to me to be based on conclusive arguments, and that the evidence points rather to the he-goat than to the ram as the chosen embodiment of the local deity.

The question would be settled immediately had we found the original contents of the coffins, of which several are still to be seen, and are known to have been there since the Middle Ages. But neither Brugsch's excavations nor mine have given us an unrifled specimen. The coffins are of black granite, and with one exception, they are uninscribed. That exception is represented by a lid, which was discovered by Brugsch, and is now exhibited in the Museum at Ghizeh.⁶ The lid was originally five feet two and a half inches long, and two feet seven inches wide; there are only fragments of it left. It did not belong to one of the largest sarcophagi, for some of them were as much as six feet long. The animal which the lid had covered is called in the inscription 🜚 *Ba ankh, the living soul or the living spirit.* The bird with a human head 🜚 *ba*, is here a variant of the ram 🜚 to be

---

³ Lib. ii. 42. ⁴ *Zeitschr.*, 1877, p. 8.

⁵ Tochon, *Médailles d'Égypte*, pp. 63, 167; J. de Rougé, *Monnaies des Nomes de l'Égypte*, pp. 11, 46.

⁶ Mariette, *Mon.*, pl. 42-46.

found on the Ptolemaic tablet. I think, therefore, that the expression of the tablet must be translated *the living soul* or *the living spirit*, rather than *the living ram*. The coffin is ornamented like sarcophagi for human beings, with representations of the sky, of the gods of the elements, of night and day, and of the different hours, and with the name of each of them. The words spoken to the *Ba ankh* are quite similar to the formulae addressed to men. The sacred ram is supposed to symbolise the productive and generative power of nature, and he unites in his own person four different rams, who are sometimes represented in an abridged form as one single body with four heads. On the Ptolemaic tablet he is called: *the King of Upper and Lower Egypt, the living spirit of Ra, the living spirit of Shu, the living spirit of Seb, the living spirit of Osiris, the spirit of spirits, the lord of lords, the heir in the city of Tonen* (Mendes). In another part of the same text it is said of him: *appearing on the horizon with four heads, illuminating heaven and earth, coming as Nile, causing the earth to live, and (giving) the air to mankind.* From these two texts it is clear that he is supposed to unite in himself the four elements, light or fire, water, earth, and air; these are the four heads with which he is often represented, or the four different rams of the composite deity, which are sometimes attributed to four different cities of Egypt.

But whether the sacred animal of Mendes was a ram or a he-goat, it was, at any rate, treated as a god, and divine honours were granted to it. The ram lived in the temple, and had his priests and his priestesses, who took care of him. As with the bull Apis, there was only one sacred ram at a time, one having certain characteristic marks in proof of his divinity. Like Apis also, he appeared somewhere quite unexpectedly. In the Ptolemaic tablet it is said that in a year of Ptolemy Philadelphus, which was probably the twenty-second, people came to say to His Majesty that a ram had appeared in a certain locality west of Mendes, near the pylons, and they asked that the king himself should enthrone the god, and establish him in the temple, the repairs of which had just then been completed. Five experts were called in to examine the animal from cities where it was worshipped; and when they had duly inspected the young ram, and certified that his marks were correct, according to the divine regulations, his fourfold title was given him, the king himself enthroned him, and caused him to be led in procession into the temple. A great festival took place; and the king availed himself of the occasion to dedicate a statue of his deceased sister and wife Arsinoë, which was to be placed near the sacred ram.

As I said before, the city of Thmuis superseded Mendes when Egypt was under Roman rule. The name of Mendes does not occur in the list of bishoprics, but only that of Thmuis. ⲐⲘⲞⲨⲒⲤ ⳨ ⲂⲀⲔⲒⲞⲘⲞⲨⲒ are the names we find in the Oxford list.[1] The great quantity of Roman ruins, aqueducts, remains of barracks and of what I consider to be the palace of the governor, which had a portico with granite columns, all show the importance to which the city rose under the Romans. I dug in several of the houses without finding anything valuable. I have elsewhere described the chambers filled with burnt papyri, which I called the library of Mendes, but which should more correctly have been described as the library of Thmuis. Whether it was a library, or merely held the archives of the city, it certainly contained a considerable number of documents. A few fragments in possession of Daninos Pacha have been read by Prof. Sayce, who found them to be accounts. But it is probable that in a building of such a large extent there must have been books of another kind. They were all written in Greek.

---

[1] J. de Rougé, *l.c.*, p. 156.

THE NOME OF THOTH.

On the same side as the mounds of Tmei el Amdid, but nearer to Mansoorah, the traveller passes another mound close to the present station of Baklieh. A few years ago he might there have seen a number of fellaheen actively engaged in excavations, under cover of getting "sebakh" manure for their fields, but really looking for antiquities. Now the mine is exhausted, the mound has been partly levelled to the ground, and, even for a fellah, there is no further use in working there.

In traversing the short distance which separates the station from the mounds, we first reach a space covered with enormous blocks of black granite (pl. xii. A.) and red limestone. Among them are two capitals in form of a lotus flower, only roughly hewn and not yet polished. One of them has been split in two, for, as usual, this heap of big stones has served as a quarry. Evidently a king of Egypt—whose name we do not know, but who, judging from this building material, which is very like that of Behbeit, might be a king of the XXXth Dynasty, or even a Ptolemy—intended building a temple here. To that end, he brought hither stones from Upper Egypt, but was afterwards obliged to give up his project, owing to circumstances also unknown to us.

This heap of stones stands near the opening of an enclosure-wall built round an area of a few acres, containing the remains of the old city, which could not have been very large. It probably possessed but a small sanctuary, which was to be renewed or enlarged. At a short distance from the large mound is a smaller one, where the fellaheen have been digging for years, until parts of the mound have completely disappeared. It was a necropolis of sacred ibises, and the spot has long supplied the shops of antiquity dealers in Cairo with bronze heads and figures of the sacred bird. All over the tell lay heaps of bones of the bird of Thoth, and the figures were thrown among them exactly as in the case of the cats of Bubastis. Some mummified ibises were found in cases made out of a kind of cement. Along with the remains of these birds were found one or two sarcophagi of white limestone, which were immediately broken up, and also a few statuettes, one of which is dedicated to Thoth, and is now in the British Museum.

The presence of so many ibis relics naturally led to the idea that this was the site, if not of the capital, at least of one of the cities of a nome dedicated to Thoth, Hermes, and which might have been called Hermopolitan by the Greeks. In the hope of discovering the name of the place, I cut extensive trenches all through the mound, but notwithstanding their number and their depth, I did not come upon the trace of any important buildings whatever. Evidently, if there had been a temple, it was a small building which soon disappeared, and which was to be replaced by a larger one for which the necessary material had been brought from Upper Egypt. Besides, in the heart of

SITE OF HERMOPOLIS.

the Delta the people are far from any quarry. It is not easy to get limestone there, and the smallest piece found on the tell would speedily have been carried away. That seems to be the reason why there are hardly any remains to be seen there, excepting big blocks of granite, for which there is no ordinary use.

Such fragments of inscriptions as I found were discovered in the village of Baklieh; they are four in number. The first is a piece of limestone, the lower part of a door-post, on which are the following signs: ... *worshipper of the great, the lord of Bah.* The second is a fragment of hard stone used as the threshold to the tomb of a sheikh of a neighbouring village (pl. iii. B.). The inscription is of the time of Nectanebo II., and states that the king was a worshipper of Thoth. Probably the name of the city in which Thoth is said to reside immediately follows upon the name of the god, and this supposition might easily have been verified had the Arabs allowed me to remove a brick of the door-post covering a few inches of the stone. But after having remained there a long time, after having tried all kinds of argument, even that which is to them the most persuasive of all arguments—the sight of gold, I failed to overcome their obstinacy. They feared to irritate the deceased saint, who would deeply resent any damage done to the door of his tomb, and who would cause his wrath to be felt. So I was obliged to go away without the sight of those few signs. A third fragment is a large piece of a basalt coffin which I had taken out of a mill. The name of the deceased was *Anhmes*. He had several titles, the most important of them being lit. *the baldheaded*, the title of one of the high-priests of the XVth nome of Lower Egypt, the nome of the ibis, or of Thoth. The names which I found on these inscriptions all point to that nome in which the ibis was worshipped, and this is in good accord with the fact of the sacred birds' having had their necropolis at Baklieh.

The name of the nome of the ibis would lead us to think that this was the Hermopolitan nome of the Greeks, and that its capital was Hermopolis Parva, known to have been in the Delta. But it is not so; we do not know of any Hermopolitan nome having existed in the Delta, whereas the city of Hermopolis Parva in Lower Egypt is spoken of several times. The name occurs three times in Strabo, and it is probable that the Greek geographer meant two different cities.[1] Of the first, he says that it was on the river near Lake Mareotis, and also that it was on an island near Buto. Evidently this was the city which Ptolemy had in view, when he says that Hermopolis was the metropolis of the nome of the Alexandrians.[2] That city was on the site of the present town of Damanhoor,[3] and by far the most important city of the name in Lower Egypt, probably much more important than its Greek namesake in the eastern part of the Delta. I believe that the eastern Hermopolis, which would be far more correctly entitled to the name of "city of Hermes" than the western one, is also mentioned by Strabo, who says that it was situate in the country above the Sebennytic and the Phatnitic mouths, along with Lycopolis and Mendes. It is quoted also by Stephanus Byzantinus, who speaks of a city of Hermopolis κατὰ Θμοῦιν,[4] near Thmuis, and lastly by the geographer of Ravenna, who also

---
[1] Pp. 802, 803.
[2] Ἀλεξανδρέων χώρας νομὸς καὶ μητρόπολις Ἑρμοῦ πόλις μικρά. P. 123, ed. Bert.
[3] D'Anville, *Mém. sur l'Égypte*, p. 70. It is difficult to understand why the Greeks called Hermopolis a city dedicated to Horus and not to Thoth.
[4] The only edition I have now at hand (1568) reads κατὰ Ῥομοῦν, an evident mistake. The article in Pauly, *Real. Encycl.* reads κατὰ Θμοῦιν.

quotes an Ermopolis immediately following Theomis,[5] which is evidently Thmuis.

The Egyptian cities had each so many names that there is nothing extraordinary in our finding various localities with the same name when it was translated into Greek or Latin. There are several places called Iseum, Serapeum, Diospolis, because they worshipped the same divinity. The reverse may also occur in other instances, considering that the Greeks followed no definite principle in their rendering of Egyptian names. For some reason unknown to us, and apparently quite arbitrary, although two places had the same god, they might be differently named by the Greeks,—perhaps in order to avoid confusion. I believe this to have been the case here. Although the nome of Thoth is not given by Ptolemy as Hermopolitan, it was known to him and its position is indicated in his work. I quite agree with M. J. de Rougé,[6] that we must recognize it as the nome called *Νεούτ*, *Νεοnt*,[7] whose capital was *Panephysis*, or *Panithusos* as it is called in Hierocles.[8]

This nome of *Νεούτ*, Ncout (ΝЄϹΥΤ on the coins), must, according to Ptolemy, have been in the immediate vicinity of the nome of Mendes.[9] The origin of the name *Νεούτ* is not known, but as for that of the capital, if we adopt the reading of Hierocles, Panithusos, we may find in it a corruption of the name of Thoth, 𓏺𓈖𓅝 *Pa en Dhuti, the house of Thoth*. The Coptic has preserved the tradition of the worship of Hermes in the name[1] ⲛⲓⲙⲁⲛⲑⲱⲟⲩⲧ, *the places of Thoth*, which is said to belong to the diocese of Thmuis.

Let us now turn to the hieroglyphic inscriptions and see what information they afford as to the nome of Thoth. The lists give us three names which may refer either to the capital, or to the more important cities of the province: 𓉐𓏤 𓅝 𓎟 𓂋𓐍𓎛 *Pa Dhuti ap Rehuh, the house of Thoth the judge of the Rehuh*; 𓅝 𓊖 *the city of Thoth*; 𓏤𓊖 with many graphic variants, *Bah*, which we found at Baklieh. I believe that we must add to these three a fourth, 𓏤𓏤𓏤𓊖 *Shmun*, which has always been interpreted as referring to Hermopolis Magna, in Upper Egypt, but which in my opinion must also be applied to the Hermopolis near Mendes. Certain monuments evidently coming from Lower Egypt bear the name of Thoth of Shmun, as for instance a cynocephalus in black granite, about one foot high, which I saw in a farm not far from Baklieh, and which was doubtless dug out of one of the mounds of the nome of Thoth. On its base are these words : 𓀀 𓏏 𓎛𓊪 𓏤𓏤𓏤𓊖 *Praise given to Thoth the lord of Shmun*. It would be extraordinary if this Shmun applied to the city of Hermopolis Magna, so far away from the spot. Besides, we see that Thoth 𓊖 𓏤𓏤𓏤𓊖 *who resides at Shmun*, occurs among the gods of Lower Egypt[2] who assembled at the great festival celebrated by Osorkon II. at Bubastis. Hence it seems to me probable that the capital of the nome of Thoth in Lower Egypt was also called *Shmun* 𓏤𓏤𓏤𓊖, like Hermopolis Magna, the capital of the XVth nome of Upper Egypt. I consider that another name of the capital of the nome of *Νεούτ* is 𓅝 𓊖 *the city of Thoth*, and 𓉐𓏤 𓅝 𓎟 𓂋𓐍𓎛 *Pa Dhuti Ap rehuh. Ap rehuh, the judge or the guide of the Rehuh*, is also one of the usual titles of the Egyptian Hermes. We find him called by that name in the sculptures of the hall of Nectanebo I. at Bubastis, where are represented many divinities

---

[5] Ed. Pinder et Parthey, p. 126, Nos. 11 & 12.
[6] *Geogr. de la Basse Egypte*, p. 105.
[7] Νεοὺτ νομός, καὶ μητρόπολις Πανέφυσις (p. 124, ed. Bert.).
[8] P. 727, ed. Wesseling.
[9] D'Anville, *l.c.*, p. 92.
[1] Champollion, *L'Egypte sous les Pharaons*, ii. p. 120. Zoëga, *Cat. man.*, p. 18.

[2] *The Festival Hall*, pl. viii., p. 21.

of Egypt, and where he is shown as standing next to *Hamehi*, the goddess of Mendes.³

On the other hand, I consider that *Bah* ☥ ☉ was not the capital, but some other city of the same province, and I have no hesitation in assigning to it the site of Baklich, from the temple of which came the fragment bearing that name, and also the sarcophagus with the characteristic priestly title.

If *Bah* is at Baklich, I believe that the capital of the nome, *the city of Thoth, the house of Thoth Aprehuh* or *Shmun* as it was called, is to be looked for in the mounds of Tannah, a place often referred to by the natives of Tmei el Amdid. It is about seven miles north of Mendes, and ten miles east of Mansoorah. The fellaheen say that monuments have been found there, and at a short distance from it is the village called *Ashmun er Rummân*, which, as Champollion rightly observes,⁴ must not be translated Shmun of the Romans, but Shmun of the Pomegranates. According to the same author, this place was called also *Ashmun Thannah*.⁵ It is probable that the cities built on the sites of Baklich and Tannah were separated from Mendes by the Mendesian branch of the Nile, which bounded the nome of Thoth on the south-east.

I have already mentioned that close to the tell, near the opening in the enclosure wall, there is a large heap of unworked blocks intended for the building of a temple to be erected on that spot, and that these blocks seem to be of the kind of material which would have been employed by the XXXth Dynasty. It is remarkable that we should have a record which may refer to this very temple. In the quarries of Toora, south of Cairo, Brugsch⁶ discovered an inscription stating that Nectanebo II. "opened a good quarry at Toora, in order to build in good stone a sacred abode to Thoth Aprehuh, the great god of Bah, and to the gods of Bah." From Toora he could only get limestone, and none of the black granite which comes from Hamamât in Upper Egypt. But we may conclude from this inscription, that since he intended to build a temple, he would also, when sending the limestone from Toora, order the granite blocks and capitals which were to adorn the halls and the gateways of the buildings to be brought from the upper country. But the grave events of his reign, and the abrupt termination of his rule, prevented Nectanebo from carrying out his plans.

A monument, which would be interesting if complete, is the basalt sarcophagus of which we have only a fragment. The sculpture is clearly of the Saïte style; moreover, the dead man's name of *Aahmes* is another indication of the same period. Aahmes, or as the Greeks would have called him, Amasis, had different titles. He was first ♀. Whether the second sign is to be read ☉ ⎯⎯ *ma, the river-side, the shore*, or ☉ ∨ *tep, the field*, it seems that he had in either case the superintendence of land. The same office appears to be implied in the predicate added to his priestly title ⎯⎯ ⎯⎯ *the fek, the bald-headed on the earth, or on the land*.

As for the title of ⎯⎯ ⎯⎯, we know from the lists that it belonged to the priests of the nome of Thoth; but the word ☉ generally means *on the earth, living*, in opposition to the buried. Here, however, it is clear that it has another sense. These words must also refer to land, and probably mean that the *fek* Amasis was specially entrusted with the supervision of the land belonging to the temple. A third title, which is very vague, is ⎯⎯ *superintendent of the temples*. We do not know what this title really meant, and whether it gave any authority to the bearer; it may have been merely honorary, and

---
³ *Rubastis*, pl. xiv. v.
⁴ *Egypte sous les Pharaons*, ii. p. 124.
⁵ Champollion, l.c., ii. p. 152, 351.   ⁶ *Zeitschr.*, 1867, p. 91.

only indicative of a certain rank in the hierarchy. I am inclined to think that if it refers to a real employment or office, it denotes a man who has to look after the building itself, its walls, and everything connected with construction and repairs.

On the upper register of the sarcophagus were figures of the protecting genii of the deceased during the hours of night and day. The lower register gives the names of the hours. On the side which has been preserved we have the names of the second, third, fourth, and fifth hours of the day. The hours of the night were probably given on the other side. It is to be observed that these few names completely differ from those of the lists known up to the present time,[7] even from those in the list given by a Saïte coffin of the Leyden Museum. On the Baklieh sarcophagus, the names seem to have been engraved with the greatest carelessness, and by an artist who evidently did not understand what he was inscribing. He had to engrave on a given space an inscription consisting of the following parts: the number of the hour of the day, its name, and these words: *protecting thee Osiris*, etc., with name and title. As the space was very limited, he nearly sacrificed the second part, shaping the name of the hour according to the room which was left, omitting many signs and putting in others which had no sense. The second hour is called ⬚ *ptarheh, seeing millions*. This name is correctly written, but it generally applies to the third hour. The third, ⬚, seems to me to have no meaning at all. Perhaps the last signs ⬚ are taken from the usual name of the second hour, which ends with the word *the night*, ⬚, and ⬚ are only inserted to fill up the space. As for the name of the fourth, ⬚, I believe that the engraver mistook for the name of the hour what is nothing but an unusual way of writing "fourth," ⬚, found on the coffin of the sacred ram from Mendes.[8] A good style of sculpture and beautifully engraved characters are not always the guarantees of a correct text, especially in later times. As at Mendes, so too the Saïte sovereigns built at Baklieh. The only cartouche which I discovered there is of Psammetichus II. It is on a piece of limestone (pl. iii. *c*), which was also built into the walls of the mill-pond from which I took the fragment of the coffin.

---

[7] Brugsch, *Thes.*, p. 843.

[8] Mariette, *Mon.*, pl. xlvi.

LEONTOPOLIS.

One of the most beautiful parts of the Delta is the region south of the city of Mit Ghamr on the right side of the Damietta branch of the Nile. There, the lofty date-palms, the magnificent sycamore trees overshadowing the villages, the splendid gardens where peach and almond-trees are in full blossom in the month of March—all these natural beauties attract the eye of the traveller and bear witness to the rich fertility of the soil of Egypt. In the midst of this fine country, about six miles from Mit Ghamr, rise extensive mounds known as *Tell Mokdam*, and covering an area of several hundred acres. In spite of the constant digging for sebakh, they have not yet been reduced as much as many others. Patches which have never been touched tower to a height of more than sixty feet, and the whole mound is a labyrinth of hills and valleys through which it is difficult to find one's way.

Tell Mokdam has been known for many years. Excavations were made there in Mariette's time, and the fellaheen digging for sebakh had come across an old cemetery among the houses. Two inscribed coffins of late epoch were found. One of them, a very large one in black granite, is still on the spot. The natives also discovered the base of a statue in black granite, which is now in the Ghizeh Museum, where it was brought last year by Count d'Hulst, at the expense of the Fund.

The coffin gives several geographical names,[1] but we are uncertain as to the Egyptian nome to which they belonged. The place seems to have been called ⟨hieroglyphs⟩ *Iakhennu*, and to have had as divinities Osiris under the form of a lion, called *Arihes*, and *Amon*. The fact of the lion's being worshipped there gives probability to the view expressed by several writers to the effect that we must consider it as being the site of the *Leontopolis* of Strabo, the more so since the Oxford list of bishoprics gives Saharagt as the Arabic equivalent of the Coptic names ⲖⲈⲞⲚⲦⲒⲞⲚ, ⲖⲀⲒⲰⲚⲦⲰⲚ.[2] The present village of Saharagt el Koubra, on the Damietta branch of the Nile, about twelve miles from Benha, is close to Tell Mokdam. It is from Saharagt that the Tell is best reached, coming from the south. We do not know with certainty to which nome this city must be attributed. It does not seem to have been the capital of an Egyptian province, though it was certainly a provincial capital in the time of the Antonines, since there are nome coins with the name of Leontopolis.[3] They bear either a lion or a man holding a lion in his hand. I agree with M. J. de Rougé that Leontopolis probably formed part of the nome of Athribis, now Benha.

It is to this city that we must apply the information found in Aelianus, as to the worship of lions in Egypt. He says that "in Egypt lions are worshipped, and there is a city which derives its name from that animal . . . the lions have temples and numerous habitations . . .

---

[1] Mariette, *Mon.*, pl. lxiii.

[2] J. de Rougé, *Géogr.*, p. 155.

[3] Tochon, *l.c.*, p. 169; J. de Rougé, *Monnaies*, p. 47.

every day meat of oxen is offered to them, and while they eat people sing to them in Egyptian." If there were sacred lions at Leontopolis, it is to be expected that some day, in parts of the Tell which have not yet been excavated, or at least somewhere in the neighbourhood, a necropolis of those animals will be found.

The attention of Mariette and other Egyptologists was directed to Tell Mokdam chiefly owing to the discovery made there by the fellaheen of the base of a statue in black granite, bearing near the feet the cartouches of a king who was supposed to be a Hyksos, because it was thought that his name began with the sign of the god Set, the divinity worshipped by the foreign invaders. Devéria, Ebers, and others have considered him as being the Shepherd king called Salatis by the chronographers. This name is not the original one; it is not the first engraved upon the statue, it is that of an usurper. The monument, judging from the style of the sculpture, must be attributed to the XIIth or the XIIIth Dynasty. It was left on the spot where it was discovered until last year, when it was removed to the Museum at Ghizeh at the same time as two other bases were sent to Europe. But the cartouches which were engraved on each side of the feet have been published by Devéria[1] and by Mariette.[2] In comparing these two publications with mine (pl. iv. n.1 n.2), it would seem, if they are correct, that the monument had suffered mutilation since it was first found. All inscription on the left side has disappeared from the group ☥ which preceded the cartouche; even the goose ☥ is gone. We have lost a cartouche which was quite illegible, and the words ⌬ who worships the lord of Avaris. I am rather inclined to think that there may be a mistake in these publications, and that these words which were thought to be the end of the left line belong to the back of the statue, where the son of Rameses II., Merenphthah, engraved a dedication to Set of Avaris. The monument bears no traces of recent mutilations. On the occasions of my two visits to Tell Mokdam, in 1885 when I came to see the place, and in 1892 when I settled there to excavate, the monument was almost entirely buried in heaps of potsherds, and I suppose this has been the case ever since it was discovered. Besides, it would be extraordinary to find the city of Avaris, the capital of the Hyksos, mentioned in an inscription which is older than the Shepherd Kings. And after having made several paper casts of the monument, and studied it attentively, I found out that the reading of the name is quite different from what it was supposed to be. The name reads thus: ☥ Nehasi, the Negro. The mistake arose partly from the ☥ which is behind the bird ☥, and which, as the characters are not very distinct, was taken for the tail of Set, and partly from the two crests on the head of the bird, which are not unlike the two ears of the typhonic animal.

The name Nehasi has been found in other places. In the list of the Turin papyrus it is borne by a king who belongs to the XIVth Dynasty, and it was also found at Sân by Prof. F. Petrie[6] as that of *a royal son, the first-born, the worshipper of Set the lord of Roahtu* ☥. It is natural to think that the three names refer to the same man,[7] that the royal son of Sân, the negro who raised buildings

---

[1] *Rev. Arch.*, Nouv. série, vol. iv., 259.
[2] *Mon. divers*, pl. 63. The sides are inverted in both publications.

[6] *Tanis*, i., pl. iii.
[7] It is remarkable that in the Turin papyrus, and on the stone at Sân, we find the unusual spelling noticed here, ☥.

to Set, was afterwards the king of Tell Mokdam who worshipped the same god; and as he was the first-born of the royal family, it is clear that he came to the throne by inheritance as legitimate king, and not by right of conquest. I have dwelt elsewhere* on the conclusions which may be deduced from this fact. If we consider what was the history of the XIIth Dynasty, and also that of the XIIIth, as far as we know anything of the reigns of the Sebekhoteps and Neferhoteps, there is no doubt that most of their campaigns were directed against the Nubians and the Ethiopians. The negroes and the peoples of the Upper Nile must have been more formidable enemies than we supposed, otherwise it would not have been necessary to make war so constantly against them, and to erect those fortifications which may be seen to the present day, in places like Semneh. There would be nothing strange if in those troubled times, the history of which is so obscure, Egypt had been for a time under the rule of Ethiopian negroes. This view would agree with the tradition recorded by Herodotus,⁹ who says that between Menes and Moeris, who dug the lake bearing his name, there reigned three hundred and thirty monarchs, whose names the priests read to him from a papyrus, and that among them there were eighteen Ethiopians. However unreliable we may think the figures of Herodotus, it is curious that the number of Ethiopian kings should have been so large; and it is quite possible that there may have been negro kings like Nehasi, of whose existence we were ignorant, especially as they are not likely to have raised many monuments, or to have left extensive and faithful records of their reigns. It would be extraordinary that a king of the XIVth Dynasty should call himself a negro, if he did not belong to the Ethiopian race.

* *Transactions of the IXth Cong. of Orientalists. Recueil de travaux*, vol. xv., p. 97.
⁹ Lib. ii., cap. 100.

The site of the temple at Tell Mokdam is clearly discernible on the eastern side of the tell. It is now a cornfield. I dug several trenches there, but they yielded no results beyond a few fragments of limestone, showing that the temple ruins had shared the fate of those at Baklieh, and of most of the sites of ancient cities in the Delta. There could not have been much granite in the building, as that would have been at least partially preserved.

On the north side, at the end of the mound, towards Mit Ghamr, in digging for sebakh, the fellaheen had discovered, shortly before I arrived, the base of a statue in red limestone, which they immediately broke in two. I dug in the same place, and found remains of statues of Rameses II. and Osorkon II. in red granite, and another base, also in hard red limestone. The two monuments in limestone have been brought to England; one of them is now in the British Museum. They both consist of the lower parts of sitting statues of Usertesen III., one of the greatest kings of the XIIth Dynasty. Their workmanship is remarkably good, the hieroglyphs are beautifully cut, and the little that remains of the female figures represented as standing on each side of the throne, against the legs of the king, shows that both statues must have been of great beauty. This only increases our regret that such fine works of art should have suffered most wanton mutilation. One of the seated figures is of natural, and the other of heroic size (pl. xii. c). The smaller one has been usurped by an officer of Osorkon II., while the larger one bears the name of Usertesen III. only.

An examination of these statues indicates that they were made for the temple which stood at Tell Mokdam. The king is said to be a worshipper of Osiris, who, as we know from the inscription on the sarcophagus, was the local deity of the place, and there assumed the form of a lion. Moreover, in front of the feet of one of the bases stood the name of a god which has been destroyed, but which had for determinative a lion-headed figure. The name of Osiris is on the belt of the larger statue, followed by a geographical name which I could not make out (pl. iv. A). It is remarkable how many statues and monuments of the XIIth Dynasty have been discovered in the course of excavations in the Delta, especially on the eastern border. Tanis, Nebesheh, Bubastis, and other places of minor importance were settlements of the Amenemhas and the Usertesens. Some of them may have been bulwarks against the Asiatics.

On the large statue we see the nine bows on which the feet are resting. On both sides of it the titles of the queen have been fairly preserved, but not her name (pl. iv. A.). Almost the identical titles are found on a stele at the Louvre,[1] and there they evidently apply to a person raised to royal rank by her marriage with a member of the royal family. The name itself is no longer legible, so that the wife of Usertesen III. is still unknown to us. On both sides of the two statues are the Nile gods of Upper and Lower Egypt holding a rope tied around the sign ⚱ which means to *join*; they are here emblems of the land of the North and the land of the South, and are supposed to promise to the king eternal life and happiness. The belt buckle of the statue bears the name of Usertesen, and states that he is the worshipper of Osiris.

The smaller statue is more interesting because it was usurped in the name of Osorkon II. by an officer of the name of *Hormes* (pl. iv. c. 1—5). The usurpation has been made with great carelessness. On the sides, the cartouches of Osorkon II. have been cut over those of Usertesen, without the engraver doing anything to erase the older ones; hence the two cartouches are confused. On the back two columns of text give us the name and titles of Osorkon II.

These titles are here given even more fully than at Bubastis. The words 𓏏𓆇𓏤 *who joins the two halves, like the son of Isis*, meaning both parts of Egypt, which are determined by the two diadems, I also found on a fragment of a statue in red granite, which may have been made for Osorkon II.

The titles of the officer who usurped the statue for his master are interesting. We see that he was *holy father of Amonrasouter*, which perhaps shows that there was also a sanctuary of Amon at Leontopolis. He held another office, which I do not understand, and which also referred to "the lord of the gods of Egypt." It may have been that of chief of the officers who had to superintend the ornamentation of the temples. Besides, he was head of the sanctuaries, and had it in his charge to repair the temples of Egypt. This last title is very general, it may have referred to a merely nominal employment. Another of his offices was connected with the temple of the city; he was *governor of the house of millions (of years) of Osorkon II.* Here we have the name of the temple where the statues were erected. I should think that it was built by Osorkon, who brought thither some older statues. Whether there was a library in the temple or not, Hormes was *head inspector of the book-writers of the king*.

In the temple called *the millions (of years) of Osorkon II.* there was a hall or sanctuary specially dedicated to his queen. It was called *the house of the royal wife Karoumam*. We have repeatedly seen this queen accompanying Osorkon II. in the inscriptions of Bubastis, especially among those of the festival. She certainly was his legitimate wife, and although at Thebes Osorkon had Theban wives, connected with the priesthood and the worship of Amon, in the Delta we find mention of no other than Karoama. It is not impossible

---

[1] Lieblein, *Dict.*, No. 349.

that she was dead when he built the sanctuary at Tell Mokdam, and that he deified her, even as later on Ptolemy Philadelphus deified his sister-wife Arsinoë. It is to be noticed that here we find her name written ⌒⌒⌒ *Karoamama*, whereas in the inscriptions at Bubastis, where her name occurs so often, we never find the final ⌒.

Again, at Tell Mokdam, though on a smaller scale, we find further proof of a fact which was so strikingly brought into evidence by the excavations at Bubastis. The two Osorkons, who until a few years ago were thought to have been obscure kings governing a weak and impoverished country, and having great difficulty in defending their throne against invaders from east and west, now stand out as wealthy monarchs, fond of erecting temples and great buildings, and who made magnificent gifts to the gods of the land. This could not have been so unless the kingdom had been at peace and prosperous. It was not under the Osorkons that the great decadence took place which is so marked under the XXIIIrd and XXIVth Dynasties. If it began at all under the Bubastites, it was only under the later ones.

In the sanctuary which he built to Osiris and to his queen, Osorkon collected other statues than those of the XIIth Dynasty. There was the base of a standing statue of Rameses II., in red granite, with his cartouches and titles repeated several times, even on his belt. Everywhere among them we find this epithet, ⌒⌒⌒ *beloved like Phthah*. It would have been strange if, amid the ruins of a sanctuary containing statues, there had not been found at least one monument bearing the name of Rameses II.

APPENDIX.

BYZANTINE SCULPTURES FOUND AT AHNAS.

The accompanying illustrations are copies of some beautiful photographs (taken by the Rev. William MacGregor) of various sculptures found in Egypt amongst the Mounds at Ahnas by M. Naville, who was conducting excavations there for the Egypt Exploration Fund.

Ahnas is about seventy-three miles south of Cairo, and occupies, no doubt, the site of Heracleopolis Magna.

A description of it was given by the late Miss Amelia B. Edwards in the special report of the Fund, 1890-1891, and it is further described by M. Naville in a letter which he has been kind enough to send to me, of which I subjoin extracts, so far as it relates to the sculptures. He says: "The site of Ahnas consists of several mounds, between which are depressions, in which generally stood the stone buildings. In one of these were two large bases of columns in red granite, which evidently appeared to be of late Roman or Byzantine times. In digging at the foot of these bases, I found a large architrave and pieces of the columns which stood on those bases, but, as there were only two, it must have been a gateway leading into the church. I was quite certain that the building was a church when I saw the heap of stones found lower down at a depth of eight or nine feet. I say a *heap* of stones, for, from the state of the ruins, it would have been impossible to reconstruct the plan of the building, except that the apse seemed to have been raised on a platform of burnt bricks, to which access was given by a flight of steps. The stones consisted of a great number of lintels, friezes and cornices in white limestone, with sculptured ornaments, the motives of which are flowers, leaves, and heads of animals, chiefly sheep and hogs. . . . Besides these were bases of columns in grey marble, shafts of the same material, and capitals, noticeable from the fact that the central flower in the abacus is replaced by a Coptic cross. . . .

"There are the remains of two other churches, which consist merely of shafts of columns of red granite. On some of these the Coptic cross has been engraved, and these columns look exactly like those at Medinet Haboo and in other well-known Coptic churches. They are all of the same kind of work. As for the standing columns and Corinthian capitals, called Kanesch, the church, I believe they were originally parts of a Roman temple. The style of the capitals seems to me to have less of the Byzantine character which is so strongly marked on the others, especially in the flat capitals which are at the top of the square pillars to the church."

I am informed that these sculptures, thus described by M. Naville, are now the chief objects in one of the Coptic rooms at Ghizeh.

I was there last in 1890, but I cannot recall them to mind. I have, however, now before me the elaborate work in folio by Mons. Gayet, published in 1889,[1] describing such sculptures as were then in the Museum, and classed by M. Maspero as Coptic. A glance at them will show not only that they are deplorably deficient in merit as compared with those from Ahnas, but are from an entirely different school. But in classing them all together as Coptic, the Museum authorities would probably include all Christian sculptures in Egypt, from whatever school they might have come.

A few of M. Gayet's engravings show, indeed, some fair Byzantine work, and in some few of the others, viz., in the scroll-work, there is some approach to elegance of form; but the greater part, where any attempt at composition has been made, are the rudest imitation of Roman work.

The attempts at sculpturing the figures of birds, beasts, &c., and the human form, are often quite ludicrous, and so are many of the imitations of Corinthian capitals and other details.

But now, thanks to our energetic explorer, M. Naville, and to the excellent photographs of Mr. MacGregor, we find that the sculptures of the Egyptian Christians may take rank with some of the best of the Byzantine period.

I can, in fact, scarcely call to mind any Byzantine carving which is superior to that at Ahnas. The curves in the scroll-work are very graceful, and the foliage, although rather tame in design, is as clearly and boldly cut as in the beautiful works at Constantinople, Ravenna, or Torcello; whilst the representations of animal life, as shown in the birds (pl. xiv.), and the boar and kid (pl. xv.), are very well carved, and are introduced in the most artistic manner.

The large Corinthian capital (pl. xvii.), although in the debased Roman style, is fairly well copied from the antique. This being so,

[1] *Mémoires de la Mission Archéologique Française au Caire.* Tome troisième. 3° Fascicule. Paris, 1889.

it is somewhat vexatious to find that there are scarcely any portions of the Ahnas sculptures (except the capitals to the columns and and pilasters) to which one can assign any definite position in the building. They were, I understand, put together as shown in the illustrations, so as to be most easily photographed.

M. Naville has no doubt that they formed portions of the ornamental work to a church; but the plan of the building, so far as one can judge of it, appears to be very different from that of the usual *Coptic* church.

The rough sketch which I here give has been worked out with the kind assistance of Mr. MacGregor, the parts shaded being those which exist.

The apse was not placed in the usual easterly position, but was slightly east of due *north*, the entrance columns being slightly west of due *south*. The apse had also its circular form showing externally, contrary to the ordinary rule.

Further, it will be noted that only one apse, or position of the altar, is described by M. Naville, whereas three eastern altars are required by the Coptic ritual, and I am assured by Mr. MacGregor that there is no trace of the two side altars having existed.

On the whole, I think that it is fair to conclude that this interesting building was not originally designed for the Coptic service, and that Mr. MacGregor's suggestion is a very probable one, viz., that it was a small chapel like that to the White Monastery, of which a small plan is given by Mr. A. J. Butler,[2] reduced from that given by Denon, and which faces north and south, with an apse to the north, resembling in both these features the little church of Ahnas.

This White Monastery is said to have been founded by St. Helena; and from the glowing descriptions which Mr. Butler quotes from Mr. Curzon and M. Denon, we may, I think, fairly conclude that much of the substantial fabric of the monastery chapel now remains as she left it.

The feature in the photographs which will attract most attention is the headless figure with lion, shown in pl. i., and, as I felt the importance of this, I consulted with Mr. A. S. Murray on the subject, and he has been kind enough to send to me his conclusions, viz., "That this sculptured group must have represented Orpheus, whose appearance is not uncommon, apparently, in the early Christian art of Italy. The photograph shows a draped figure seated to the front, and holding at his left side a lyre, which his right hand has been stretched across to play. On the right is a lion springing towards the lyre in a Mycenian attitude. Very probably there was another animal similarly posed on the left. It would, probably, be nearly correct to go back to the fifth century as the date of the chapel at Ahnas."

The carved work over the lion, and the very peculiar way in which the lower part of the drapery of Orpheus ends, serve to identify the figure with the style of the other portions of carving, and we may, I think, class them all as being of a date at least as early as the fifth century, the date which Mr. Murray gives for the Orpheus.

The carving has the peculiarly sharp cutting of the Byzantine sculptors, and much of it has the well-known character of that style, so that I should not hesitate to class the whole as Byzantine; but much of the scroll-work is bolder and more graceful in outline than I am accustomed to meet with in examples in other countries, and certainly conveys to my mind the impression that possibly Byzantium owes its decorative carving, as Mr. Butler suggests that it owes its domical designs, to Egypt, and that M. Naville has thus brought to light the earliest example of Byzantine art yet known.

T. HAYTER LEWIS.

[2] *Ancient Coptic Churches in Egypt,* vol. i. p. 352.

November, 1893.

INDEX.

	PAGE
Aahmes, priest	23, 25
Aakhennu, locality	27
Abode, the eastern	6
,, the good	6
Aboosir	4 note, 19
Abul-'Abbás Ahmed, geographer	16
Acacia	6
'Ad, locality	16
Aelianus	27
Ahnas	1, 2, 11
,, el Medineh	2
Aken, canal	19
Alexandria	18
,, nome of	23
Alexandrian calendar	9
Amasis, king	17, 18
Ambassadors	3
Amenemha III.	11
Amenophis III.	12
Ament	13
Ammianus Marcellinus	16
Amon, god	9, 19, 20, 27, 30
,, horns of	20
Amonrasonter	30
Anuaref, sanctuary	7, 8
,, god	10
Anrudef, sanctuary	6, 7, 8
Anubis, god	13, 14
Ἀνύσις	4
Antoninus, Itinerary of	16
Apis, bull	21
Apries	18
Arihes, god	27
Arsinoë	21, 31
Arsinoïte nome	4
Arsaphes, see *Hershef*.	
Ashmun er Rummán	25
Ashmun Thanuah	25

Asiatics	
Assurbanipal	
Atef headdress	
Athribis	
Avaris	
Ba ankh, god	
Baba, god	
Bah, city	
Bahr Yusúf	
Baklich	
Bald-headed, the, priest	
Behbeit el Hagár	
Behnesa	
Benha	
Beni Suef	
Bes, god	
Bindidi, city	
Book of the Dead	
British Museum	
Brugsch, Prof. H.	
Brugsch-Bey, E.	
Bubastis	
Burton	
Busiris	
Buto	
Calasirians	
Caracalla	
Chabas, F.	
Champollion	
Cisterns	
Coffin, basalt, at Baklich	
Coptic churches	
Cynocephalus	
Damanhoor	
Damietta branch	

INDEX.

	PAGE
Daninos-Pacha	21
Daphnae	3, 4
Delta	3, 4, 15, 17, 23, 27, 29, 30
Denderah	9
Dévéria, Th.	28
Dillmann, Prof.	3, note
Diocletian	16
Diospolis	24
parva	20
Duemichen, Prof.	3, 4, 11
Ebers, Prof.	28
Edfou	9
Elements, the four	21
El Moudid	15
Ermopolis, see Hermopolis	
Ethiopians	29
Ezekiel	15
Fayoom	2, 11
papyrus of the	6, 11
Feshn	5
Firmament, raising of the	8, 9
Gebel Ahmar	16, 18
Ghizeh, museum at	18, 20, 27, 28
Girard	17
Griffith, Mr. F. Ll.	1
Groeber, Mr. H.	18
Hamamât	2, 25
Hamehi, goddess	19, 25
nome	19
Hamenna, official	12
Hanes	3, 4
Harabchent	4
Harmakhis	7, 10
Harpocrates	19
Haru, priest	19
Hathor	14, 19
capital	18
Hawara	6
Hawk	7
He-goat	16, 19, 20
Heliopolis, see also *On*	9
Henassieh	1
Henassieh el Medineh	1
Heracleopolis magna	1, 2, 3, 4, 5, 6, 7, 8, 11
island of	4, 5, 6
kings of	1

	PAGE
Heracleopolis, nome of	4
parva	16
Heracles	7
Hermopolis parva	23
magna	24
nome of	7, 22
Herodotus	4, 7, 15, 16, 19, 20, 29
Hershef (Arsaphes)	1, 2, 6, 7, 9, 10, 11, 14, 20
house of	16
Hierocles	24
Hor, officer	9
Hornes, officer	30
Horus, god	6, 8, 9
neb ma kheru, the justified	7, 10
Horufa, priest	19
Hotepka, official	14
Hours of day and night	26
Hun, canal	6, 11
Huneb, god	9
Hunensu, Huncusulen	2, 8, 9, 10, 14
Hunt, woman	13, 14
Hunuri, priestess	14
Hyksos	28
Ibis	22, 23
Illahun	2, 6
Iphicrates	15
Isaiah	3, 4
Iseum	24
Isis	6, 30
Islands	4, 5
inner	6
Israelites	3
Jomard	4, 16
Josephus	15
Kantarah	16
Karoamani, queen	30, 31
Kenisch, church	1
Khataaneh	11
Kheui, official	2
Khens, locality	4
Khernoter	13
Khininsi, city	3, 4
Khnum, god	7, 20
Kom el Dinâr	1
Leontopolis	15, 27, 28, 30
Lepsius, Prof.	20

INDEX.

	PAGE
Library of Thmuis	21
Libya	4
Lion deity	27
Louvre Museum	30
Luxor	5
Lycopolis	23
Ma, goddess	9, 10
Macarius, St.	16
Mamelukes	1
Mansoorah	22, 25
Mareotis, lake	23
Mariette	2, 27, 28
Marseilles, museum at	5
Maspero, Prof.	1, 2 note, 10
Melaha, village	1
Memphis	16
Mendes, city	3, 15, 16, 17, 18, 19, 20, 23, 25, 26
coins of	20
nome of	15, 19, 21
god	19
Mendesian branch	15, 25
Menes, king	29
Menkheperra, king	12
Memnont, locality	11
Mer, mountain	6
hoo	13
Merenphthah	10, 18, 28
Merutensa, official	2
Mesen, locality	6
Military caste	15
Mit Ghamr	27, 29
Mœris, lake	5, 6, 7, 11
king	29
Mohammed Ali	1
Murray, Mr. A. S.	18
Murtâhia, province	16
Nar, sanctuary	6
Neboshoh	30
Nebkara, king	2
Nectanebo I.	24
II.	15, 23, 25
Negroes	28, 29
Nehasi, king	28, 29
Neôŕ	24
Nile, the	4, 5, 6, 11, 15, 21
Upper	29
Nilometer	6
Nilopolis	4

	PAGE
Nomus	19
Nubians	29
Oleander	6
Omm el Kemân	1
On, Heliopolis	10, 18, 19
Oppert, Prof.	3
Osiris	6, 7, 9, 10, 13, 21, 29, 30
anneru f	10
Hershef	8
Osorkon II.	24, 29, 30, 31
Oxyrynchos	5, 16
nome of	5
Pa lat neb Dad, Mendes	19
Pa en Dhuti, Hermopolis	21
ap Rehuh	21, 25
Palestine	15
Pan as Mendes	16, 19
Panephysis, city	21
Panithusos, city	24
Pa usar neb Dad, Busiris	19
Pennsylvania, University of	11
Persian troops	15
Petrie, Prof. Fl.	2, 28
Phamenoth, month	9
Pharnalazus	15
Phatnitic mouth	23
Phileas, Bishop	16
Phœnix, sacred	9
Phthah	31
Piankhi, king	6
Ploughing, festival of	9
Plutarch	7, 19
Pottery	12, 14
Psammetichus II.	18, 26
Ptolemy, geographer	4, 5, 6, 15, 23, 24
Ptolemy Philadelphus	24, 31
Ra, god	6, 8, 9, 10, 21
Ram	7, 17, 19, 20, 21
Ramses, scribe	14
Rameses II.	2, 9, 10, 11, 14, 18, 28, 29, 31
III.	10
Ravenna, geographer of	23
Rouhtu, locality	28
Roba	18
Tell	15
Rohenun, Hamamât	2
Roset	9
Rougé, Vic. J. de	24, 27

INDEX.

	PAGE
Saharagt el Kombra	27
Saladin, sultan ...	5
Salatis, king	28
Saltpetre pits ...	1
Samanood	19
Sand, he who is on his, god	7
Sayce, Prof.	21
Seab, Temple	6
Sebakh ...	1, 22
Seb, god ...	17, 21
Sebennytos ...	3
Sebennytic branch	15, 23
Sed, periods ...	9
Sekhet, goddess ...	8
Semneh ...	29
Serapeum ...	24
Serapion, bishop	16
Set, god	6, 7, 8, 9, 28, 29
Shephont, priestess	19
Shunu, city ...	24, 25
Shrine of Mendes	16, 17
Shu, god ...	8, 9, 17, 21
Simbillaonin	15
Sioot ...	1
Sokaris, god ...	13
Spoons, carved ...	12
Ssedment ...	5, 14
Gebel...	11
Stephanus Byzantinus ...	23
Steward, high	2
Strabo ...	4, 5, 15, 19, 23
Suez canal	16
Suidas	19
Superintendent of the temples ...	25
Tanis, Sân ...	3, 16, 28, 30
Taouah	25
Tahraka Tirgú, king	3
Tell Ibn es Salâm	15
Tell Mokdam ...	27, 28, 29, 31

	PAGE
Temi, mound	15
Tesh, region ...	6
islands of ...	6
Thebes ...	1, 4, 5, 20, 30
Thoumis, city	24
Thmuis, city	15, 21, 23, 24
Thoth Aprehu	25
Thoth, god	7, 22, 23, 24, 25
nome of ...	22, 24, 25
the city of	24, 25
the places of	24
month	6
Titus	15
Tmei el Amdid ...	15, 19, 22, 23
Tombs at Ssedment	11-14
Tonen, god ...	8
city of	21
Phthah	9
Toora, quarries of	25
Tum, god	7
Tumei, locality ...	16
University College, Egyptian museum at	13
Usertesen II., king	2, 10
III.	29, 30
Usheldis	12
Ut'a, sacred eye...	12
Version of the Bible, revised ...	3
Chaldæan	3
Vestibule...	9
Vineyards ...	9
Wasta	4
Yusûf	5
Zaweh ...	4
Zeús, Amon as	19
Zoan, see Tanis ...	3

INDEX TO APPENDIX.

BYZANTINE SCULPTURES FOUND AT AHNAS.

	PAGE
Ahnas, Byzantine chapel of	33, 34
,, ,, ,, compared with that of White Monastery ...	33-34
,, ,, its columns, pillars, and capitals ...	32, 33
,, ,, ,, its probable date ...	34
,, described by Miss Edwards	32
,, ,, M. Naville	32
,, site of Heracleopolis Magna	32
,, three churches of	32
,, position of	32
Apse, single, of Byzantine chapel	33
Apses, three, of Coptic churches	33
Butler, A. J., his plan of White Monastery	34
,, ,, his *Ancient Coptic Churches in Egypt* ...	34
Coptic churches, characteristics of	32, 33
,, cross at Ahnas	32
,, sculptures at Ghizeh ...	32, 33
Corinthian capitals at Ahnas ...	32, 33
Gayet, M., his work on sculptures in Museum at Ghizeh	33
Helena, Empress, founder of White Monastery	34

	PAGE
Kaneseh, or "church," at Ahnas	32
Lewis, T. H.	34
Lion, sculptured figure of, in Mycenean attitude	34
MacGregor, Rev. W., his description of Byzantine chapel	33-34
,, ,, his ground-plan of ditto ...	33
,, ,, his photographs of the sculptures	32, 33
Murray, A. S., on sculptured group of man and lion at Ahnas ...	34
Orpheus, in Early Christian art ...	34
,, sculptured figure of, at Ahnas	34
Roman temple, remains of, at Ahnas ...	32
Sculptures, the, Byzantine character of	33, 34
,, ,, now at Ghizeh	32
,, ,, probable date of	34
,, ,, subjects of ...	32, 33, 34
White Monastery, its chapel compared with Byzantine chapel at Ahnas	33-34

CONTENTS OF PLATES.

Frontispiece. General View of the Temple discovered at Ahnas. Phot. Rev. W. MacGregor.

PLATE I. A.B. Inscriptions on the entrance to the Temple (pp. 7, 10).
   C. Side of a Statue of Rameses II. (p. 11).
   D.E. Stray Blocks with Standard of Usertesen II. (pp. 2, 10)
   F. Group of Priest and Priestess (pl. XII. B., p. 14).
 II. Columns of the Vestibule (pp. 7, 10).
 III. A.B.C. Inscriptions from Baklich (pp. 23, 25, 26).
   D. Inscription from Tmei el Amdid (p. 17).
 IV. A.C. Statues of Usertesen III. discovered at Tell Mokdam (p. 30).
   B. Cartouches of Nehasi (p. 28). *Ghizeh Museum.*
 V., VI. Columns and Architraves from the Vestibule of the Temple at Ahnas (p. 10). Phot. Rev. W. MacGregor.
 VII., VIII. Mummy Cases from the Necropolis at Ssedment (p. 13). Phot. Rev. W. MacGregor.
 IX. Pottery from the same Necropolis (p. 14). Phot. Rev. W. MacGregor.
 X. A.B. Statue of Rameses II. presented to the University of Pennsylvania [1] (p. 11).
   C. Unknown Head (p. 11).
 XI. Mummy Cases from the Necropolis at Ssedment (pp. 13, 14).
 XII. A. Baklich, Heap of Stones for an unfinished Temple (p. 22).
   B. Group of Priest and Priestess found at Ssedment (p. 14). *Ghizeh Museum.*
   C. Statue of Usertesen III. found at Tell Mokdam (p. 29).
 XIII. Map of the Mound of Ahnas. Drawn by Prof. Erman.

APPENDIX.
XIV.-XVII. Byzantine Sculptures from Ahnas.

[1] The Photographs of Plates X.-XII. were taken by the author.

PLATE I.

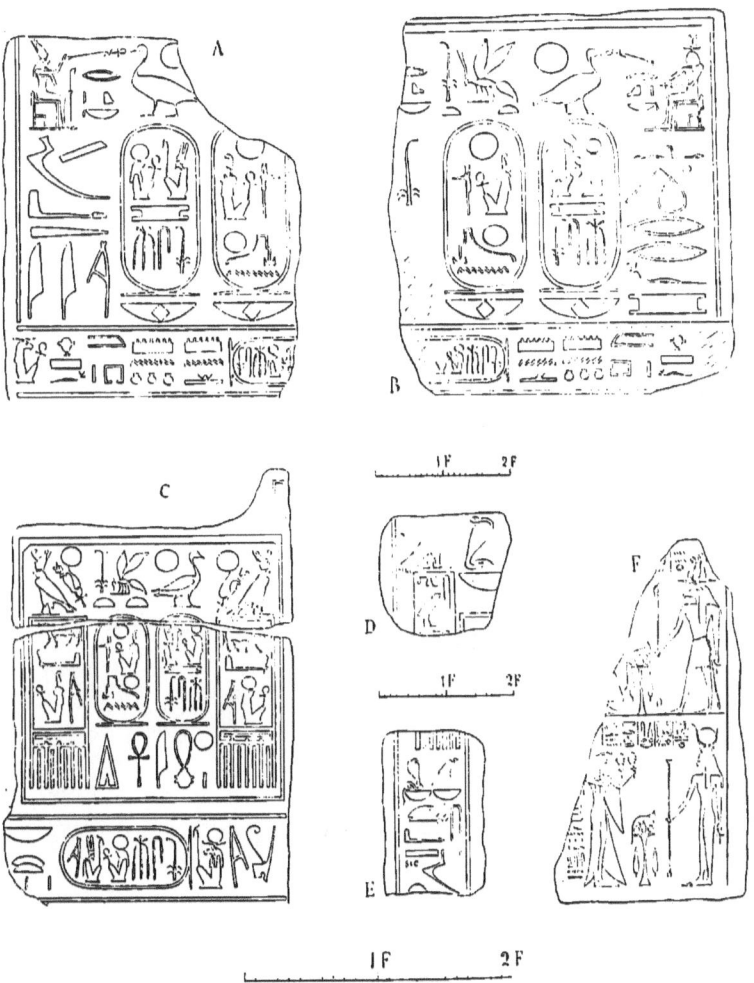

HERACLEOPOLIS.

INSCRIPTIONS ON ENTRANCE OF TEMPLE (A, B) ON STATUE OF RAMESES II. (C);
ON STANDARD OF USERTESEN II. (D, E); ON GROUP OF PRIESTS AND PRIESTESSES (F)

PLATE II.

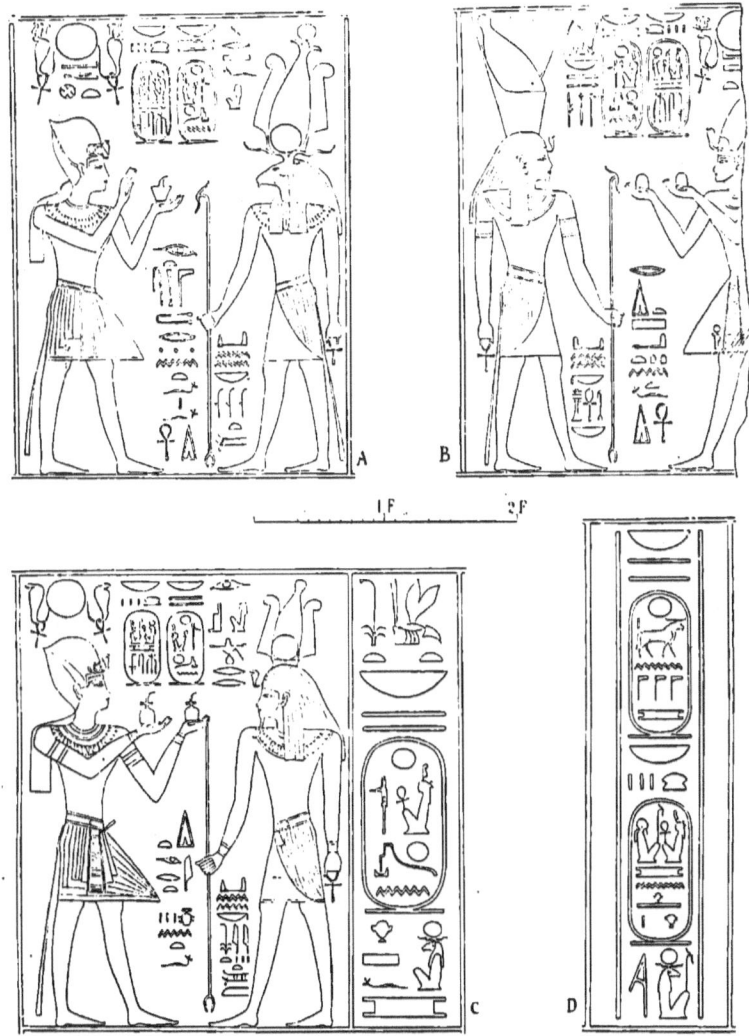

HERACLEOPOLIS.
COLUMNS OF THE VESTIBULE

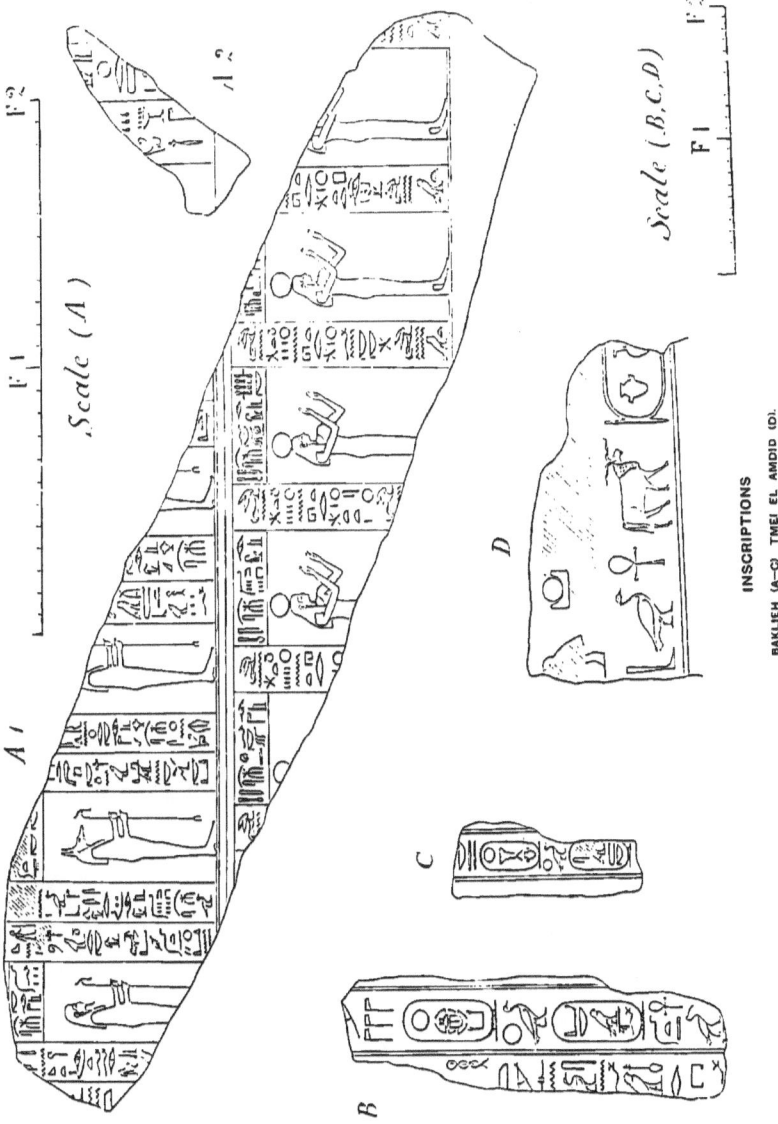

INSCRIPTIONS

BAKLIEH (A-C) TMEI EL AMDID (D).

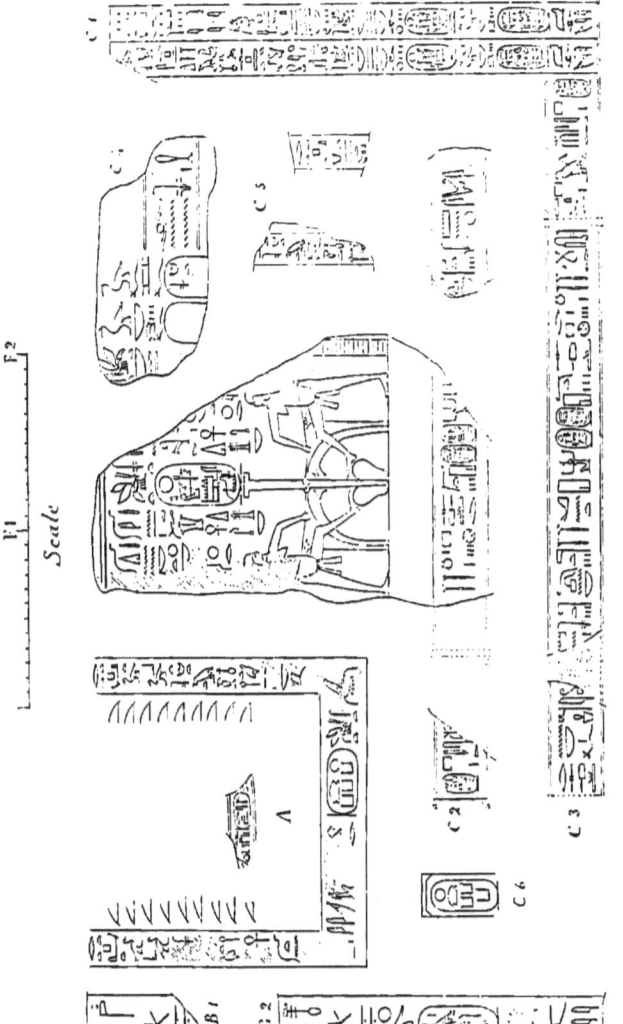

TELL MOKDAM.
STATUES OF USERTESEN III. (A, C) CARTOUCHES OF NEHASI (B).

HERACLEOPOLIS.
COLUMNS AND ARCHITRAVES FROM THE VESTIBULE OF THE TEMPLE.

HERACLEOPOLIS.

COLUMNS FROM THE VESTIBULE OF THE TEMPLE.

MUMMY CASES FROM THE NECROPOLIS AT SSEDMENT.

PLATE VIII.

MUMMY CASES FROM THE NECROPOLIS AT SSEDMENT.

POTTERY FROM THE NECROPOLIS AT SSEDMENT.

PLATE X.

A

B

C

HERACLEOPOLIS.
STATUE OF RAMESES II. (A, B); UNKNOWN HEAD (C).

B

C

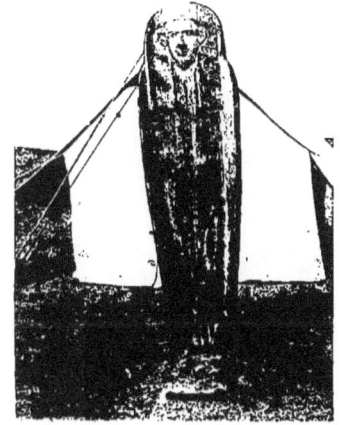

MUMMY CASES FROM THE NECROPOLIS AT SSEDMENT.

PLATE XII.

BAKLIEH (A). PRIEST AND PRIESTESS: SSEDMENT (B).
STATUE OF USERTESEN III.: TELL MOKDAM (C).

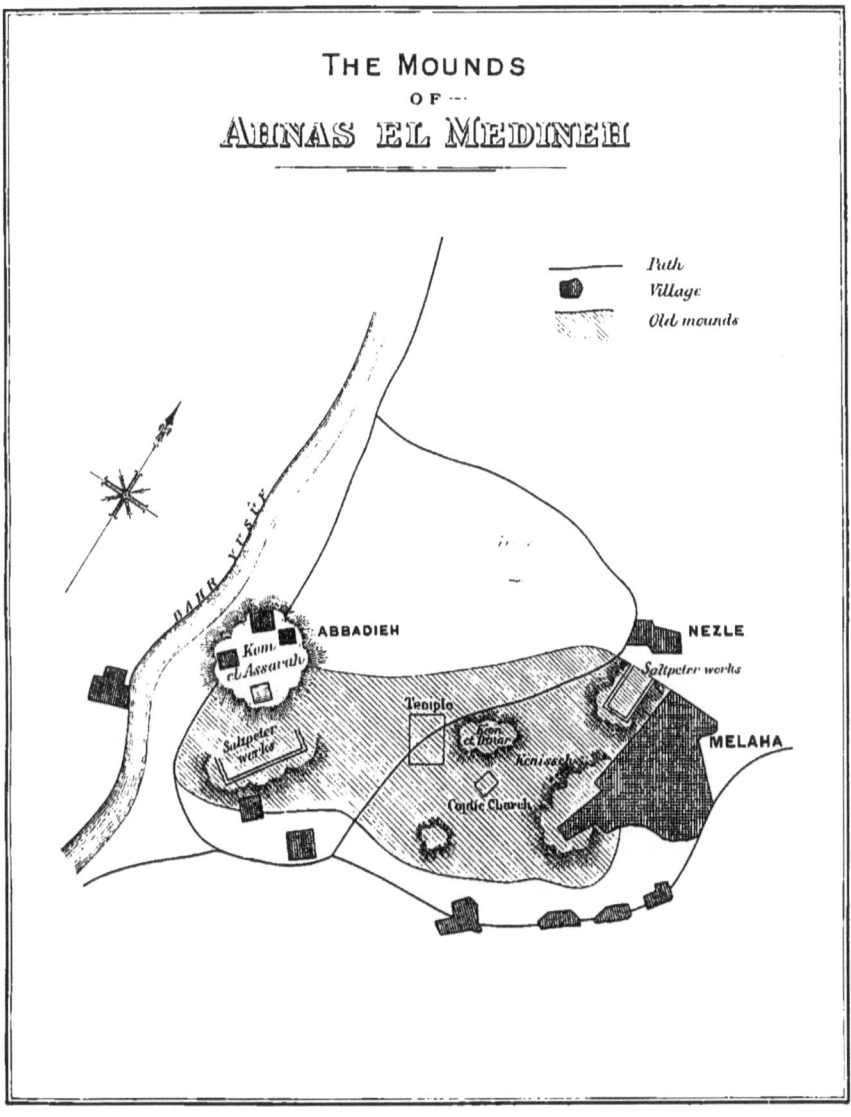

BYZANTINE SCULPTURES FROM AHNAS.

BYZANTINE SCULPTURES FROM AHNAS.

BYZANTINE SCULPTURES FROM AHNAS.

PLATE XVII.

THE
TOMB OF PAHERI AT EL KAB.

PREFACE.

The Committee of the Egypt Exploration Fund, taking advantage of the liberal offer of Mr. J. J. Tylor to place at their disposal a selection of his drawings from the tombs of El Kab, decided to provide the subscribers with a complete delineation of that of Paheri, one of the most representative examples existing of its period (the middle of the XVIIIth Dynasty). Notwithstanding that numerous details from the tomb have already appeared in the great works on Egyptian monuments, there has never been any approach to a complete publication of the scenes and inscriptions.

Mr. Tylor's materials lent to the Society for this purpose were—

(1) An admirable collection of photographs, the negatives of which were taken for him by Mr. Harold Roller in 1892. They are as follows, all except the first four being to the scale of one-sixth actual size :—

View of the interior of the tomb, from the entrance.
Two views of the façade, and one of the side wall, scale 1 : 16.
Two photographs of the fragment that remains of the front wall.
A series of fourteen photographs of the left side of the main chamber.
A similar series of the right side.
A series of seven, of the inscriptions on the back wall.

(2) Tracings of the scenes on the sides of the niche, which could not be photographed.

(3) Annotated copies of the above photographs.

(4) Drawings based on enlargements (to nearly double the scale) of most of the photographs of the scenes. These enlargements were made in order to serve as a basis for Mr. Tylor's own *édition de luxe*.

The plates in the present volume were prepared as follows :—

Pls. vi., vii., and the inscription on the back wall in pl. ix., were first traced from the original photographs by a draughtsman, and then carefully corrected and completed. The drawing of the statues on pl. ix. is derived from that in Lepsius' *Denkmäler*.

Pls. i.-v. and viii. were traced from the enlarged drawings: this method was calculated to give more satisfactory results, owing to the abundance of detail in the scenes. The services of Mr. Anderson, a skilful draughtsman, especially practised in the delineation of classical subjects, were engaged for this work.

Pl. x. is from a drawing founded upon Mr. Tylor's tracing. It has been compared with the copies published in Lepsius' *Denkmäler*, but does not pretend to absolute accuracy of detail.

All the above have been subjected to careful revision, by close examination of the photographs and comparison of numerous published and unpublished copies. The method adopted has been to draw the reliefs in outline, and to fill in the incised work in full black. Restorations have been inserted only so far as they are authorized by the direct evidence of the earlier copies; and in all cases the outlines of the more recent fractures have been clearly marked within the restorations, so as to indicate their extent at the time that the photographs were taken.

No plans of the tomb could be found, excepting a very small and inaccurate one published in the *Description de l'Égypte*. Fortunately, Mr. Somers Clarke, F.S.A., who was in Egypt with Mr. Tylor in 1892, had taken some measurements, which he was good enough to communicate to the authors, together with some remarks upon the architecture. From these, with the help of the photographs, a useful sketch has been possible, and is shown upon pl. i.

The present memoir does not represent the final outcome of Mr. Tylor's work upon the tomb of Paheri. He is now engaged upon a limited *édition de luxe*, in which the scenes will be reproduced to a larger scale by a collotype process. His drawings for this work are based upon the photographs, and are intended to render the effect of the reliefs in a more natural way than has ever before been attempted.

In conclusion, the Committee of the Egypt Exploration Fund desire to express their extreme obligation to Mr. Tylor for the generous manner in which he has placed his materials at their disposal and for the share which he has taken in the preparation of this memoir.

CONTENTS.

	PAGE	PLATE
I. INTRODUCTION—		
1. General description of the tomb of Paheri	1	I. (plan)
2. Previous work at the tomb	3	
3. The nomarch Paheri	5	
4. Genealogical tables	7	
II. EXPLANATION OF THE SCENES AND INSCRIPTIONS—		
1. Façade and wall at side of entrance	10	I.
2. Front wall	11	II.
3. West wall	12	
South end : the official life of Paheri	12	III.
Centre : Paheri's unofficial life and amusements	17	IV.
North end : funerary scenes	19	V.
4. East wall	22	
North end : the banquet	23	VI., VII.
South end : worshipping the gods	25	VIII.
5. Longitudinal inscriptions (frieze and ceiling)	26	III.-VIII.
6. Back wall and niche	27	
Back wall	27	IX.
Statues in the niche	32	IX.
Sides of niche	32	X.
INDEX	33	

THE
TOMB OF PAHERI AT EL KAB.

I. INTRODUCTION.

1. GENERAL DESCRIPTION OF THE TOMB OF PAHERI.

THE ruins of the ancient city of Nekheb, now El Kab, lie on the edge of the Eastern desert, and form a square of about half a mile in each direction, clearly defined by an immense fortified enclosure of crude brick. It was an important city, worthy of its position as capital of the IIIrd nome of Upper Egypt. At some distance to the north-east of the enclosure is a rocky mass of sandstone honeycombed with tombs, and separated from the cliffs behind it by a narrow gulley: this was the main necropolis of the place, and on its southern slope are some interesting tombs, chiefly of the period of the New Kingdom. The first and the most striking of these is the tunnel-like sepulchre of Paheri, dating from the middle of the XVIIIth Dynasty.

The dimensions of this tomb, however, are but moderate, the main chamber being only 25-26 feet long and 11½ feet broad. The original excavation comprised[1] a levelled platform before the entrance, in which the mummy pit was sunk; a sculptured façade; an oblong main chamber with arched roof, decorated throughout with sculpture and painting; and finally, a niche or shrine at the inner end of the last, containing three statues.

At a later period a neat doorway was cut through the sculptures of the East wall, and two rough-hewn chambers, with a mummy pit, were added. The floor of the main chamber appears also to have been quarried away to some depth, leaving irregular masses in the corners; while the façade in its ruinous condition now affords a wide entrance, which lights up the whole of the interior.

The façade of the tomb[2] was cut back in the slope of the hill, leaving a level platform with an almost vertical face of rock on either flank: on the left this rock-face was insignificant, and was perhaps dressed away to free the approach from that quarter, but on the right the wall was broad and high, and displays a figure of Paheri, carved in *cavo relievo*, kneeling and looking outward, while he pronounces an adoration to the local goddess Nekhebt—a solar deity, and mistress of the South. The façade itself is about 14 feet wide, with the slight "batter" or slope from base to summit that was usual during the New Kingdom. The doorway in the centre of it is now entirely destroyed; it was flanked by columnar inscriptions in large hieroglyphs, with prayers for the *ka* (ghost) of Paheri, and above it were scenes of adoration.

---

[1] See Plans, &c., on pl. i.

[2] See pl. i.

Inside, the main chamber is of very simple form, tunnel-like, with straight sides and arched ceiling; its dimensions are nearly 26 feet in length, 12 in breadth, and 10½ in height down the middle; the side walls are adorned with scenes in coloured sculpture, representing on the East wall[1] banquets and worship of the gods, indoors, and on the West wall[2]—first, the out-of-door occupations of Paheri and his serfs, such as harvesting, fishing, loading ships and the like, and at the inner end the funerary rites of the time. The roof being arched, the front and back walls are rounded at the top; the former[3] shows on the right of the doorway a large figure of Paheri with staff in hand, as if about to walk out of the chamber, and in the arched portion above the level of the door a ship, the whole being surmounted by remains of an emblematic representation; but the central part over the door and the whole of the left side is destroyed. The back wall,[4] in which the niche is cut, may be compared to an enormous round-topped tablet or stela, and is almost entirely covered by a very long incised inscription in small hieroglyphs; the upper part of the curved portion is injured, but showed, perhaps, a repetition of the design at the other end, consisting of the two jackals of the North and South facing each other, and other emblems such as are commonly represented on stelæ of this age.

All of these scenes and inscriptions are raised about 18 inches above the ancient floor (which is now much quarried away), and are bordered below by bands of colour. On each of the side walls above the scenes is a line of large hieroglyphs running the whole length of the chamber,[5] and over this, at the rounded spring of the arched ceiling, there is a continuous cornice ornament of *khekers* 〈, followed by another line of large hieroglyphs. Down the middle of the ceiling runs a similar line of inscription, and the whole of the roof-spaces between the central line and each of the side lines is painted in a somewhat intricate fashion, with rows of diamonds ◇◇◇◇ formed by zigzag lines of different colours running from end to end of the tomb.[6]

The niche or shrine is raised above the floor to the same level as the scenes; it is rectangular, 5½ feet deep by 4½ broad at the ceiling, and 5½ feet high, and is without any architectural features. It contains three life-size statues[7] of Paheri with his wife and mother, seated together upon a bench against the inner wall, and looking down the tomb to the entrance: they are cut out of the solid rock in very high relief, with their names above them on the wall: as a deceased person Paheri, in the centre, with his arms on his breast, is represented as if mummified, but, like the god Osiris, retaining the flexibility of his joints and a partial use of his limbs; on the left his wife Henut-er-neheh, and on the right his mother Kem or Kam, place respectively their left and right arms at his back, as though supporting him: the features of all these are defaced. On each of the side walls[8] is sculptured a scene of offering, and above is the *kheker* ornament. The ceiling is patterned differently from that of the main chamber, but is similarly divided down the middle by an inscribed band, perhaps representing a beam which supports a mat-work roof.[9]

The added chambers need not detain us, being of later date than the tomb of Paheri.

The execution of the tomb is probably to be dated to the beginning of the reign of Thothmes III., within a few decades of 1500 B.C. The work of it is very neat and regular, but the sandstone did not offer by

---

[1] Pl. vi.-viii.   [2] Pl. iii.-v.   [3] Pl. ii.   [6] Visible in the photograph of the tomb, but not copied.
[4] Pl. ix.   [5] Shown in pl. iii.-viii.   [7] Pl. ix.   [8] Pl. x.   [9] Not copied.

any means so fine a surface for delicate sculpture and painting as the limestone of the necropolis of Thebes. The largest of the human figures in the tomb are of about the natural size. Inside, the figures, the hieroglyphs and the details are all sculptured in low relief, as well as painted, excepting that the small hieroglyphs attached to the figures in the scenes, and those on the back wall, are merely incised and filled with blue paint;[1] outside, the work is in *cavo relievo*, the better to resist injury.

2. PREVIOUS WORK AT THE TOMB.

This is by no means the first time that the tomb of Paheri has been copied or described. Ever since its first discovery on the 20th September, 1799, during Napoleon's expedition, the necropolis of El Kab, and especially this tomb, have attracted the curiosity of travellers and Egyptologists. Cortaz gives a lively description of the excitement which the discovery produced amongst the members of the French Commission, and even recounts with evident gratification the strategy which the Arabs employed to obtain inordinate bakshish from the expectant and delighted savants.[2]

While his companions made drawings of the scenes which so clearly depicted the civil life of Ancient Egypt, Cortaz was occupied in describing them. In his own words the tomb was "comme un livre que les anciens Égyptiens nous ont laissé pour nous instruire d'une grande partie des habitudes et des travaux qui composaient chez eux l'économie de la vie civile." Here for the first time were displayed the subjects of the Pharaohs as *living* persons, in that light which further discovery has made so familiar to us.

Cortaz's description is not ill done, though the decipherment of the inscriptions and the comparison of similar representations has put the task, which he undertook for the first time, on quite a different basis. The drawings by Laneret, Chabrol, Jollois, Devilliers, and Jomard might even now be of some service if other copies were not available, but they are quite as bad as most of the antiquarian drawings contained in that great pioneer work on Egypt,[3] and are only better than the wondrous sketches of monuments which diversify the pages of Norden and other travellers of the last century. Irby and Mangles, and Belzoni, who were there on August 15th, 1817, have inscribed their names between the sculptures, amongst a crowd of barbarous and ignoble signatures; but JAMES BURTON, in or about 1825, carefully copied the scenes upon the two side walls of the main chamber.[4]

In 1828 CHAMPOLLION and ROSELLINI made a stay at El Kab. The former drew up a description of the tomb of Paheri,[5] and caused

---

[1] In the plates the detailed sculpture is drawn in outline, but the small incised hieroglyphs are represented in solid black.

[2] *Grottes d'Elethyia, mémoire sur plusieurs arts et sur plusieurs usages civils et religieux des anciens Égyptiens*, par M. Cortaz, Membre de l'Institut de l'Egypte (in *Description de l'Égypte*, 2ᵐᵉ édition, Text, tome vi., pp. 97-156), and cf. Saint-Genis, *l.c.* tome i., pp. 341 ff.

[3] "On s'est attaché à copier les hiéroglyphes avec la plus parfaite exactitude"! *l.c.*, tome x., p. 72. The drawings of Paheri's tomb ("grotte principale") are published in *Antiquités*, tome i., pl. 67, 2 ; 68 (West wall corresponding to our Pl. iii.-iv.) ; 69, 1 (a funerary ceremony in our pl. v., arrival at Kher-neter), 3 (servants, our pl. vi., bottom row on left); 70, 1 (Paheri and wife with monkey, our pl. vi., on left), 2 (musicians, our pl. vii., bottom row), 3 (ship sailing, in our pl. iii.); &c.

[4] *British Museum, Additional MS.*, 25,647. The copy is excellent, but the scale (!) is too small to show much detail in a pencil drawing. Fo. 6-9, East side ; 10-13, West side ; 14 contains the end (south) of the East wall and the beginning of the West; 15, many inscriptions from both sides ; 16, musicians in pl. vii. on a larger scale ; 17, inscription over table of offerings on pl. vi., and the long lines of inscription below the frieze.

[5] Tomb 1, Champollion, *Notices Descriptifs*, i., 266-9 and 650-3.

many of the scenes to be copied;[1] the latter has published numerous scenes in his *Monumenti dell' Egitto e della Nubia*.[2]

About the same time ROBERT HAY of Linplum made a complete copy of the scenes on a larger scale than Burton.[3]

Wilkinson did but little work at El Kab. For his *Ancient Egyptians* he took only one illustration from the tomb of Paheri.[4] His description of the antiquities is to be found in the older editions of Murray's Guide.

In 1843 came the grand expedition of Lepsius, whose draughtsmen, E. Weidenbach and Eirund, have given us masterly, though conventionalized, representations of some of the most important scenes and inscriptions.[5]

In 1891 HEINRICH BRUGSCH published many inscriptions from the tomb in his *Thesaurus Inscriptionum Aegyptiacarum*.[6] Mr. Villiers Stuart devotes a chapter of his *Nile Gleanings*[7] to the tombs of El Kab, and gives a coloured plate of the musicians on the East wall of the tomb of Paheri. Professor Petrie copied all the personal names in the tombs in 1887, and doubtless every Egyptologist has added to his note-book here. The useful notice in Baedeker's *Upper Egypt* (1890) ought also to be mentioned.

Of all the copies, the first places for scholarly treatment are of course taken by the publications of Lepsius and Brugsch; while none show the subjects with great accuracy, most of them are useful for some one point or other. It is clear that little change has taken place in the condition of the sculptured walls since the French discovered the tomb, and none at all, excepting the carving of additional names, till after Lepsius' visit. Before that time many details of the sculpture had been injured, e.g., almost all the faces had been mutilated, probably by the Copts, and cracks in the rock disfigured the scenes on each wall of the main chamber: probably these had been found by the original makers of the tomb, and they had patched them up with cement, and continued

---

[1] Champollion, *Monuments*, ii., pl. cxli., 1 (winnowing and storing grain, our pl. iii., top row), 2 (ships and weighing gold, our pl. iii., bottom row); cxlii., 1 (Pa-hehet offering wine to Her-ari, in our pl. vii.); cxliii., 1 (procession of coffin, in our pl. v., top row), 2 (carrying corn to threshing-floor, in our pl. iii., top row); cxliv., 1 (chariot, in our pl. iii.), 2 (stands with jars, coloured, in our pl. iii., right-hand end of second row); cxlv., 1 (offering wine to Amensat, in our pl. vii., third row); 2 (ditto to Mey, in our pl. vii., top row), 3 (musicians, in our pl. vii., bottom row).

[2] Text, *Monumenti Civili*, i., p. 127 ff. Plates, *Mon. Cir.* xxx., 3 (swine, in our pl. iii., bottom row); xxxiii., 2—xxxiv., 1 (threshing and storing grain, our pl. iii., top row); xxxix., 1 (stands with jars, in our pl. iii., second row, on right); lxxviii., 1 (serving Her-ari, in our pl. vii., top row), 2 (serving Aahmes, in our pl. vii., second row); xcv., 7 (musicians, and serving Amensat, in our pl. vii., bottom row); cx., 1, 2 (ships, and receiving gold, in our pl. iii., lower rows); cxvi., 5 (the chariot, in our pl. iii., third row); cxxvii., 2 (procession of the coffin, in our pl. v., top row); cxxxiii., 3 (nursing Prince Uazmes, in our pl. iv., top row); cxxxv., 1 (funerary scenes, our pl. v., four lower rows).

[3] *British Museum, Additional MS.*, 29,822, fo. 107, façade; 110-121, East wall; 122-33, West wall; scale of the scenes ½. It is a careful first sketch by the camera lucida, but was never revised or completed in detail, so that all remains vague. Hay seems to have previously begun a copy on too small a scale (about ¼), now in MS. 29,843, fo. 125-7 (East wall only).

[4] Third edition, by Birch, vol. ii., fig. 479 on p. 428 (flax harvest, in our pl. iii., left end of second row).

[5] Tomb I., Lepsius, *Denkmäler*, Abth. iii., Bl. 10, a (ploughing, receiving gold, ships, &c., in our pl. iii., lower half on right), a" (the chariot, in our pl. iii., third row), b (nursing Uazmes, in our pl. iv., middle top), c (threshing, in our pl. iii., top row), e (stripping the flax-heads, in our pl. iii., second row to left); Bl. 11, a, b (scenes on the walls of the shrine, our pl. x.), c (group from the family of Paheri's wife, in our pl. iv.), d (the vintage, in our pl. iv., top right); 13 a (inscription on the back wall, and statues in the shrine, our pl. ix.).

[6] Band vi., pp. 1528-1534, inscriptions accompanying the scenes of agriculture, &c., on our pl. iii.; pp. 1534-5, inscription from the banqueting scene on our pl. vii.; pp. 1536-7, part of the inscription on back wall, our pl. ix., l. 36 to end; pp. 1539-40, genealogical inscriptions from sides of niche (our pl. x.); pp. 1540-2, ditto from East wall (our pl. vii.-viii.); p. 1542, ditto from West wall, wife's family (in our pl. iv., middle); pp. 1543-4, titles of Paheri, from south end of East wall (in our pl. iii., left).

[7] Ch. xxv. and pl. xix. (our pl. vii., bottom row, middle).

the scenes over them. Instances of such a practice are frequently observable; and the decay of the cement has too often destroyed the sculpture upon it. The only important differences now perceptible in the tomb are that the old damage has been wantonly extended by chipping fragments from the sides of the fissures,[1] and three attempts have been made to cut out figures or groups.[2] For the restoration of these the numerous early copies have been of great service, so that practically nothing has been lost to this publication through the recent disfigurements.[3]

3. THE NOMARCH PAHERI.

The principal value of the tomb of Paheri to archæologists lies in the scenes with their short explanatory inscriptions; but we can gather from this tomb and from that of Paheri's ancestor, Aahmes, "son of Abana,"[4] so much concerning the family and functions of this wealthy nome-prince, that we must devote a few paragraphs to their consideration.[5]

The genealogical tables given below, nearly all of which are derived from the evidence contained in the plates of this memoir, show that there are records of no less than seven generations of Paheri's family, reaching up to his great-great-grandmother and down to his grandchildren. He was nobly descended:

his maternal grandfather was the celebrated Aahmes, son of Abana, whose biographical inscription is one of the most precious historical records of the country. Aahmes fought under each successive king of the XVIIIth Dynasty down to Thothmes I., and was a witness of that splendid growth which first cast off the foreign Hyksos yoke, and, spreading rapidly, formed the foundation of a powerful Empire in the south and east.

By his wife Apu, Aahmes had a daughter named Kem or Kam, who probably, in accordance with custom, inherited the family honours in preference to her two brothers; she married the scribe[6] Atefrura, no doubt a grandee of the Theban court, holding the office of tutor or foster-father to the prince Uazmes.[7] As yet we have no other account of Atefrura than that which is given incidentally in the tombs of his father Aahmes and his son Paheri: he had a numerous family. Our Paheri himself, or perhaps his brother of the same name,[8] constructed his grandfather's tomb. In it we read: "It was his daughter's son who undertook the works in this tomb-chamber, in making the name of his mother's father to live, the scribe (artist) of designs of the god Amen, Paheri;" and again (a prayer) "for Aahmes, son of Abana, by his daughter's son, making his name to live, the scribe Paheri, deceased (?)."[9]

It is remarkable that Paheri bears none of the ordinary list of titles—*erpâ ḥá, semer uáti*, &c.: this may indicate that he was not a courtier. There is an air of simplicity and

---

[1] See pl. iv., vii. and viii.
[2] See pl. iv. and v.
[3] Restorations have been inserted only so far as they are authorized by the direct evidence of the early copies; and in all these cases the outlines of the more recent fractures are clearly marked within the restorations, so as to indicate their extent at the time the photographs were taken.
[4] Tomb V., L., *D.* iii., pl. 12; Ch., *Not. Desc.* i., pp. 272 and 654-658 (p. 658 wrongly printed at the back of p. 661). Unfortunately, the sculptures in it were not finished.
[5] The mythological allusions in the inscriptions are numerous and important; it has, however, been deemed advisable to leave their explanation to specialists in this class of Egyptian literature.

[6] Ch., *Not. Desc.* i., 658.
[7] Pl. ix., l. 36, &c.
[8] In his own tomb, Paheri is always called the *ha-prince*, but he was also a "skilful scribe" (pl. ix., l. 45), and at his grandfather's decease he may have borne only the title of "scribe of designs of Amen." His *brother*, Paheri, was likewise a "skilful scribe;" the occurrence of two brothers with the same name and similar titles is embarrassing. For Paheri II., see the footnote 3 on p. 8.
[9] Lepsius, *Denkmäler*, Abth. iii., Bl. 12, d and a.

straightforwardness about his titles: he was no lawyer and no courtier, but a rich and business-like countryman, a nomarch, entrusted with some important functions by the king. The abbreviated titles commonly attached to Paheri's name are "the *ha*-prince and scribe," and in ordinary language, as we learn from the conversational inscriptions in the tomb, he was spoken of as *pu há*, "the *ha*-prince," or *pu ser*, "the noble."[1] He is frequently called *ha*-prince of Nekheb and *ha*-prince of Anyt. Nekheb (Eileithyiapolis, El Kab, on the east bank) and Anyt (Latopolis, Esneh, on the west bank) were the principal cities in the third nome of Upper Egypt, called 𓎛𓏏, Ten (?), and known to the classical reader as the Latopolite.[2] Probably the nome was halved, forming territories on the east and west banks attached to each of these cities, and Paheri was made prince of both, and so of the whole nome. Esneh is about twenty-two miles distant from El Kab, and their territories probably extended north and south beyond these cities. It is not certain that any of his ancestors were *ha*-princes; so far as we can tell, therefore, this honour was specially conferred by the king upon Paheri.

Such was Paheri's princedom. As a scribe, however, he was an official with influence beyond his own nome: he is called "scribe of the accounts of corn," and once, more definitely, "scribe of the accounts of corn from Ant (Tentyra, Denderah) as far as Nekheb (El Kab)[3];" he "acted and inspected in the corn-land of the south district," was "superintendent of corn-land of the south district, excellent satisfier of the desire of his master from Per-Hathor as far as Nekheb."[4]

Per-Hathor, "the house of Hathor," is a rare geographical name, and might apply to several cities in which the goddess Hathor was worshipped. Fortunately, the difficulty is at once removed by the parallelism in two of the above titles, "from Ant (Tentyra) as far as Nekheb" evidently being synonymous with "Per-Hathor as far as Nekheb." Per-Hathor is therefore a name for the famous Hathor-city of Tentyra, capital of the sixth nome of Upper Egypt; so that Paheri was scribe of the corn for a very large district, including Thebes and extending 150 miles down the river to its great western bend at Denderah. The south district 𓈖𓏏𓈉 may be a more general designation for the same region.

Paheri's father had been "the tutor or foster-father of the king's son Uazmes," and Paheri is figured once with the same title;[5] but since the scene represents the prince as a nude baby, while the children and even the grandchildren of Paheri are present, the prince Uazmes in this scene can hardly be the same as the prince Uazmes who, accompanied by his brother Amenmes, is seated opposite Atefrura and Kema in the sculptures of the shrine.[6] A son of Thothmes I. was named Amenmes, and in the fourth year of the king was heir apparent to the throne;[7] since Thothmes I. was the last king served by Atefrura's father, there can be little doubt that the first Uazmes in Paheri's tomb, with his brother Amenmes, was a son of Thothmes I.: both of these princes seem to have died young, the succession falling to Thothmes II. Unless the scene referred to at the beginning of this paragraph be a jumble of events not contemporaneous, there still remains to be identified a second prince Uazmes, who was taken in hand by Paheri himself, about the beginning

---

[1] In Pl. iii. and vi.
[2] In the temple-lists the capital of the nome is Nekheb, but in the accounts of the Roman geographers it is Latopolis.
[3] Pl. ix., l. 10.
[4] Pl. iii., lower left-hand corner.
[5] Pl. iv., middle top.
[6] Pl. x., East wall.
[7] *Recueil de travaux*, vii., p. 142.

of the reign of Thothmes III.; such is the date to which the genealogies lead us to assign the old age of Paheri.

Paheri bore also a sacerdotal title: like most *ha*-princes, he was chief priest of the deity in his capital, and is therefore called "superintendent of the priests of Nekhebt" in one passage, or simply "superintendent of priests." Nekhebt, the goddess of Nekheb, is evidently named after the city: she was a solar deity, mistress of the south, figured as a vulture, often wearing the white crown of Upper Egypt 𓋑, and was considered to be a form of Hathor. Her divine titles are mentioned several times in the inscriptions.

4. GENEALOGICAL TABLES OF THE FAMILY OF PAHERI.

Twenty years ago Prof. Lieblein[1] for the first time tabulated the genealogy of Paheri (partly from the copies of Prof. Eisenlohr), but the materials are now much more complete.

In the following tables there is very little that is at all doubtful; it is, however, conceivable that some of those who are called "brothers" and "sisters" of Paheri in the texts may be *half*-brothers and sisters, i.e. issue not of the marriage of Atefrura and Kema, as given in the table, but of some other union of his father or of his mother; and it is believed that sometimes honorary or adoptive titles of relationship were given in Ancient Egypt to companions and friends. These reservations, indeed, will not seriously affect the value of the genealogy.

As elsewhere, the great importance attached to the maternal side of the descent is evident. Amongst the ancestors, the great Aahmes is surnamed "son of Abana" (his mother), Baba likewise "son of Reant" (his mother), and Paheri's maternal ancestors and cousins are fully represented in the scenes, while the paternal side is almost entirely neglected.[2]

I. Genealogy of Aahmes, son of Abana: from his tomb.

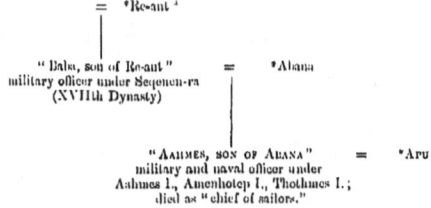

---

[1] *Dictionnaire des noms propres hiéroglyphiques*, No. 558.   [2] Cf. Petrie, *Season in Egypt*, p. 9, § 11.
[3] In these tables the asterisk (*) before a name denotes a female.

8 THE TOMB OF PAHERI AT EL KAB.

II. Sisters of Apu, wife of Aahmes, son of Abana, with their children; from the East wall of the tomb of Paheri, pl. vii.

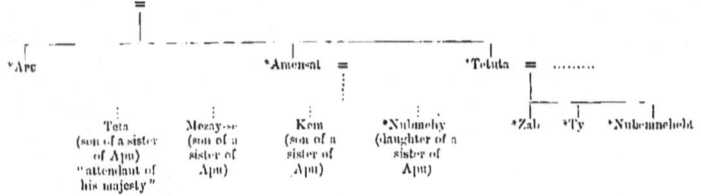

III. Children and grandchildren of Aahmes, son of Abana; from the East wall of the tomb of Paheri, pl. vii., and the east side of the shrine, pl. x.

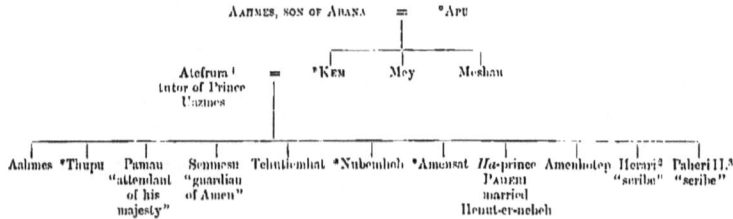

IV. Family of Henut-er-neheh, wife of Paheri; from the West wall of his tomb, pl. iv., centre.

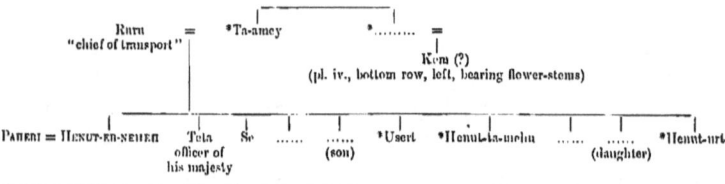

[1] Called "tutor of the king's son of his body, and scribe, Atefrura" by his son Herari, in the tomb of Aahmes, son of Abana, Ch., *Not. Desc.*, i., 658.
[2] Herari does not occur in the shrine, but is the first of Paheri's brothers on the East wall (pl. 7, top row). Like Paheri, he appears conspicuously in the tomb of Aahmes son of Abana, dedicating a scene to his father Atefrura, and his mother .... (?); his wife Amensat is with them, and he himself is called "their son who makes their name to live, the designer of the god Amen Herari," Ch., *Not. Desc.*, l.c.
[3] This Paheri is nowhere figured amongst the family of Atefrura and Kema, but is acting as scribe in pl. iii. and v., and is called "his beloved brother of the place of his heart, excellent scribe of accounts, Paheri." Probably he was an adoptive brother in reality.

INTRODUCTION

V. Children of Pahori; from the west side of the shrine, pl. x., and the East wall of his tomb, pl. vii., viii.; with his lineal ancestors, paternal or maternal.

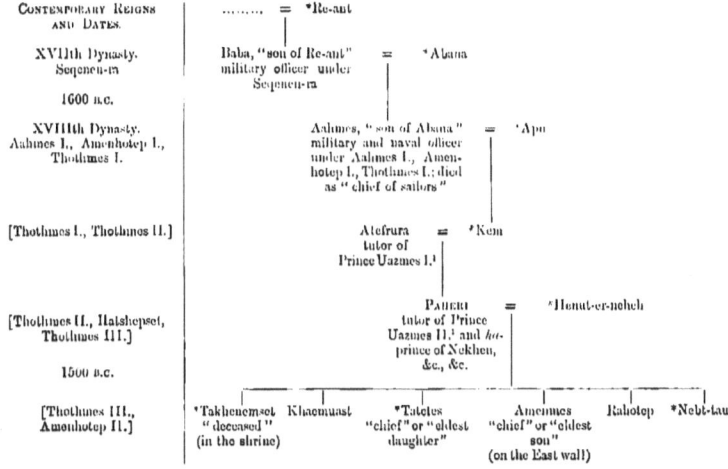

Contemporary Reigns and Dates	
XVIIth Dynasty. Seqenen-ra 1600 B.C.	.... = *Re-ant Baba, "son of Re-ant" = *Atana military officer under Seqenen-ra
XVIIIth Dynasty. Aahmes I., Amenhotep I., Thothmes I.	Aahmes, "son of Abana" = *Apu military and naval officer under Aahmes I., Amenhotep I., Thothmes I.; died as "chief of sailors"
[Thothmes I., Thothmes II.]	Atefrura = *Kem tutor of Prince Uazmes I.[1]
[Thothmes II., Hatshepset, Thothmes III.] 1500 B.C.	PAHERI = *Henut-er-neheh tutor of Prince Uazmes II.[1] and fos-prince of Nekhen, &c., &c.
[Thothmes III., Amenhotep II.]	*Takhenemset Khaemuast *Tatetes Amenmes Rahotep *Nebt-taui "deceased" "chief" or "eldest "chief" or "eldest (in the shrine) daughter" son" (on the East wall)

Grandchildren of Paheri are referred to in the tomb, and one is figured in pl. iv., top row, centre; but their names are not recorded.

---

[1] For Uazmes I. and II., see above, p. 6.

II. EXPLANATION OF THE SCENES AND INSCRIPTIONS.

PERHAPS the most instructive programme for the tour of the tomb would be, on entering it, first to visit the shrine with its statues,[1] and there make acquaintance with some of the family and ancestors of the nomarch;[2] next to inspect the festive gathering of his kin, upon the East wall;[3] then, having offered a sacrifice,[4] to "go out upon the earth" with the princely scribe as he is pictured at the entrance,[5] and be spectators of the occupations of an official and landowner as they are depicted upon the West wall;[6] after which we should follow Pahori's corpse in its funerary procession, and wonder at the strange ceremonies.[7] On the back wall we might read his lengthy and impressive epitaph;[8] and before leaving the tomb of the great man we should endeavour to repeat the prayers for his soul, while admiring the ceiling upon which they are written.

Some such arrangement may have been in the mind of the artist who designed the tomb, and that artist may have been Pahori himself. But our duty in this book is clear—it is to explain the plates, and to this end we had better take them as they come.

1. FAÇADE, &c. PL. I.

ON the Eastern wall of the entrance-platform or outer court Pahori is represented in a very simple dress, kneeling, with his arms raised towards the south. The inscription over his head is somewhat injured, but can be restored with certainty as an address to the local goddess Nekhebt, the mistress of the south :—

1. R[et [ānu en Nekhebt, sen tu en neter!]   2. ānt (?), ān [hā] mer henu neter en Nekhe]bt [....... ān] Pahēri, maā kheru: 3. [zet]-ef '[unez her-ef], nebt Re-ānti, nebt pet, henut neteru, hem nefer 4. ...... hem-ef, uzāt reyt em pet em ta, sba nefer 5. ...... en (?) [e]k-tu se............sep nefer: ȧu-nu kheret ā,.............ve-ā er mefet   7. re[ui-ā er khemt, me[t(?)-ā er ma ....el em khert heru, khent-ā 8. em ha nefer en [e]et-ui, [-et uha(?)-ā Ament nefert em khert heru ent rā neb'

"Giving [praise to Nekhebt, obeisance to] the great [goddess], by [the prince], superintendent of the priests of Nekhebt, ... the scribe, Pahēri, deceased.

"He says: '[Homage to thee], lady of Re-ānti (the mouth of the two valleys), lady of heaven, mistress of the gods, goodly helm [to him that hath no] rudder (?): balancing-power (?) in heaven and in earth, goodly star [of ....] that none sees [but in (?)] time of good ! I have come to thee............... grant me my mouth to speak, my feet to walk, my eyes to see thy [brightness] every day, that I may enjoy the good things that are given me; grant thou me to pass through the goodly Ament (West) day by day.'"

The phrases applied to the goddess are mythologically important, but are only half intelligible, owing to the lacunae. ⸺ is evidently a variant of ⸺, which is preserved in some MSS. of Burton as a title of Nekhebt in one of the temples of El Kab.[9]

---

[1] Pl. ix.   [2] Pl. x.   [3] Pl. vi. and vii.
[4] Pl. viii.   [5] Pl. ii.   [6] Pl. iii. and iv.
[7] Pl. v.   [8] Pl. x.

[9] Cf. also Brugsch, *Dictionnaire Géographique*, p. 47.

The façade has suffered severely, the whole of the doorway being destroyed; at either end are inscriptions, originally about 9 feet in height, containing prayers to various deities—

en ka en ḥá en Nekheb Paheri maá-kheru

"for the ghost of the prince of Nekheb (El Kab) Paheri, deceased." Of these the two columns on the left are a prayer to "Amen-ra, king of the gods, that he may give his pleasant breeze coming [from the North]" and other blessings, now difficult to understand in the mutilated text. On the right, in two lines, were prayers to two goddesses, and in the third line a prayer to Osiris (?) and the god of Hieraconpolis, a city opposite El Kab, on the other side of the Nile. The texts are—

(1) [*te seten hetep Nekhebt hezt Nekhen*] *nebt pet henut taui, (-es perert nebt her utch-es en khert heru ent rá neb*

prayer to "[Nekhebt, the white one of Nekhen] (?), lady of heaven, mistress of the two lands, that she may give everything that is offered upon her altar from day to day."

(2) [*te seten hetep Hether nebt set*] *usert áb, henut neteru, (-es perert nebt her khat-es en khert heru ent rá neb*

"[Prayer to Hathor, mistress of the mountain], mighty of heart, mistress of the gods, that she may give everything that is offered upon her table from day to day."

(3) Prayer to [*Usár (?) neb*] *pet Kemhes(?) her áb Nekhen ta sen khet nebt henket nebt .... nebt shesep sennu en rá neb*

"[Osiris (?), lord of] heaven and Kemhes (?) in Nekhen, that they may give all things, all offerings .... and the receiving of daily food" to the *ka* (or ghost) of Paheri."

The mummied hawk wearing the crown of Upper Egypt is read by some Kemhes. This deity gave one name to the city of Nekhen, now Kûm el Aḥmar, opposite El Kab, on the other side of the river, it being known to the Greeks as Hieraconpolis, "the city of hawks."

There were probably shorter inscriptions on the jambs of the doorway, which are now quite gone. Above are the remains of inscriptions and scenes of Paheri in adoration; these formed two rows, but they are too much destroyed for any restoration to be made of them. On the right we can ascertain that the deities adored were "[Anubis of] Ut and [Osiris of] Abydos (*Abtu*)"—

án m-ḥ áb men-kh en n b[-ef án] Paheri maá-kheru

"by the excellent satisfier of the heart of his lord, the scribe Paheri, deceased," who is now dressed in a long tunic.

The doorway probably reached to the level of the feet of the figure of Paheri.

In the passage-way, or, technically, "in the thickness of the wall," there must have existed other inscriptions; but all this is destroyed. We can now proceed to the interior of the tomb.

2. FRONT WALL. Pl. II.

On the East half of the front wall, within a border of coloured rectangles, Paheri is represented wearing a loin cloth, a thin tunic, a broad collar and armlets, holding in his right hand a napkin or handkerchief, and in his left a staff. He is proceeding towards the door—

1. *pert em ta er ma áten* .... 2. *án uá res (ep her* 3. *khert neb-ef, erf-en* 4. *ár-ef rekhut-ef* 5. *ḥá, án,* 6. *Paheri maá kheru*

"going out on to the earth to see the sun's disk .... by the uniquely watchful over his master's interests, one whose pen brought (him) his knowledge,[2] the prince, the scribe, Paheri justified."

The wall on the left of the door is destroyed. We may suppose that for the sake of symmetry there once had been a figure of Paheri corre-

---

[1] For the restoration of this and the following line, compare pl. ix., l. 1-3.

[2] Or "brought him fame (1)," cf. pl. ix., l. 27.

sponding to that on the other half, but turned in the opposite direction; in that case one figure would represent Paheri about to visit the indoor banquet and scene of offering upon the East wall, while the other would represent him "coming out upon the earth," as if crossing over to the out-of-door occupations upon the West wall.

Above the level of the lintel was an important scene with a boat, but only a fragment of it is preserved over the figure of Paheri, already described: possibly it indicated that Paheri or his ghost was prepared for a voyage on the river. Of a symbolical representation at the top of all, there remains only one sign, probably meaning *āb*, "the East."[1]

3. WEST WALL. Pl. III.-V.

Upon the West wall of the main chamber are three series of scenes. The first of these (pl. iii.) occupies nearly one-half of the total length, and represents Paheri in his public capacity as scribe and monarch, pushing forward the operations of agriculture within his district, superintending the yearly stock-taking of the herds, and receiving the tribute of gold for the king. In the second series (pl. iv.) he is in his private domain, receiving game and fish, the produce of his vineyard and gardens, and of the looms &c. in his own house. The last section (pl. v.) is occupied with ceremonial scenes from the funeral ritual. It will be observed that all the scenes on this wall are enacted out of doors.

THE OFFICIAL LIFE OF PAHERI. Pl. iii.
(1) Inspection of Agriculture and Corn.

THE greater part of the plate (more than two-thirds) is occupied with agricultural scenes, in three registers, dominated by a large standing figure of Paheri. The figure has been altered,

---
[1] Cf. the top of pl. ix.

the sculptor having made grievous mistakes about the head. Paheri was probably to be represented exactly as on the front wall, but the aristocratic wig, beard, and profile were forgotten until the stone had already been cut away irretrievably. The plebeian features are still the most prominent, in spite of the efforts made to rectify the mistake. Probably a coating of cement was laid on the surface and the head recut, partly in the stone, partly in the cement; but the latter having crumbled off, leaves the sorry sight of two profiles, two eyes, two ears and two wigs, neither face being now complete.

The inscription reads—

ma ātru ghemu ātru peri, ḥenut nebt drert em sekhet ān ḥá en Nekheb, ḥá en Anyt, drer maa en āḥt un á resi, án ḥeseb át Paheri maá kheru

"Seeing the seasons of summer, the seasons of winter, and all the occupations performed in the fields, by the prince of Nekheb, the prince of Anyt, who acts and inspects in the cornlands of the south district, the scribe of the accounts of corn, Paheri, justified."

Accompanying Paheri on his tour of inspection are three attendants bearing bags, napkins, sandals and a stool, as on the East wall;[2] one of them is the "attendant of the *ha*-prince ...... en (?)[3]

In front waits a chariot with its pair of horses of different colours; the groom Khnemem (*kazana Khnemem*) stands by holding the reins and his master's bow in one hand, and the whip in the other. The empty bow-case is seen attached to the side of the chariot. The groom endeavours to soothe and steady the impatient steeds—

áḥu em ár nezah,[4] pa ḥeter áqer, ḥá (?) mery neb-ef, ábá en pa ḥá ám-ef en hu neb

---
[2] Pl. vi., bottom row to left.
[3] The first sign in the name seems to be incorrectly formed in the original.
[4] ⸺ ⸺ (?) seems to be for ⸺ ⸺, which is found in pl. vii., speech of the servant to Sen-seubet.

SCENES AND INSCRIPTIONS.

"Stand still, be not disobedient, O excellent horse, *ha*-prince (?), beloved by his master, and of whom the *ha*-prince boasts to everybody!"¹ The construction of the chariot is very primitive, the wheel having only four spokes. Horses were no doubt still scarce in Egypt; they are found, perhaps, for the first time, amongst the hieroglyphs in the tomb of Paheri's grandfather, Aahmes, son of Abana, during the reign of Thothmes I.²

Ploughing and sowing are shown in the lowest of the three rows, reaping in the second, threshing, &c., in the first, and finally loading the corn-ships in a lower corner at the right-hand end of the fourth row. A second figure of Paheri is here introduced : as he goes down to the river to the corn-ships, he passes the ploughmen and bids them be quick.³

Two ploughs are drawn by oxen in pairs; with each is a driver, and a man sowing broadcast. They are singing—

hru nefer, tutu qebu, ua en ahu her ath, ta pet her art en ab-en, bak-en en pa ser

"A fine day, one is cool, the oxen are drawing, the heaven is doing according to our hearts, let us work for the noble!"

One of the ploughmen calls to the other in front of him—

as-tu, pu ḥati, kherp ua en ahu, mek pa ḥa ạḥa her peter

"Hasten, leader, forward with the oxen! behold the *ha*-prince is standing and looking on."

Four men are breaking up the clods with hoes. One exclaims—

khenems as-tu em baku, to-ek uḥa-en er uu nefer

"Friend, hasten at the work, let us finish in good time."

---

¹ Translations by Maspero of many of these inscriptions are to be found in the *Zeitschrift für Aegyptische Sprache*, xvii., pp. 58 ff. Others by Erman, in his *Aegypten*, and by Brugsch in his *Thesaurus*, vol. vi., pp. 1528 ff.
² L., *D.*, iii., 12, 6.
³ His speech is translated below.

To which the reply is—

auai er äet hau her baku en pa see ḳeru

"I shall do more than the work (due) to the noble : be silent (?)."

A plough of the usual form is being drawn in the opposite direction by four men with ropes, an old ploughman guiding it with both hands, and a boy sowing. Probably this is for a different crop, e.g. flax. Behind them is Paheri, who, coming down to the river to see the barges laden with corn, passes by the labourers—

uza an ḥa Paheri maā kheru er atep ua en usekhu em ta sekhet : zet-ef en ua en aḥutiu, as-ten, ta aht patet-ti, kher pa Ḥāpi āa uot

"The *ha*-prince Paheri, deceased, proceeds to load the barges in the (river-) meadow : he says to the farm-labourers, 'Hasten ye, the corn-fields are broken up (?) : the Nile was very great.'"⁴

The drawers of the plough, replying—

zet-sen āry-eu, mek-eu ; em ar seuf her ta aht, si neferta urt

"say, 'We are doing (so), behold us; fear not for the corn-fields, they are very good.'"

And the old driver, taking up the last word, exclaims—

neferui peru eu re-ek pay[-u] sheri ; renpet nefert shut em sefebu, seubet semu neb ; kher ua en behesu nefer er khet nebt

"Twice excellent is your exclamation, my son! the year is good, free of ills; healthy in all herbs; and the calves are excellent beyond anything."

In the next row above is the harvest. On the left we see the flax pulled up by men and women, the earth cleaned from the roots, and the stems tied in sheaves, after which the seed-heads are torn off with a comb. The old man

---

⁴ This must be the meaning of the passage, since no ploughing is done just *before* the inundation.

at the comb calls out to the youth who brings him a sheaf—

ȧr ȧn-ek nu 11000 *nuk se-khem-á set*

"If you bring me 11000, I am the man to strip them all." The youth answers—

as-tu em ȧr usha-re, pu áu as en áḥutiu

"Quick, do not chatter, you old *quack* of a labourer!"[1]

Beyond the flax is the corn. The reapers are at work, holding the corn in their left hands, while they cut it high up with the right. The sickles are red, of wood, the teeth white, of flint (?). One of the reapers puts his sickle under his arm, and refreshes himself with a draught of water. They are singing—

khen en uḥeb, zet-sen ' hru pen nefer per em ta ' ' ta mehyt perti ' ' ta pet her árt en áb-en ' ' bak-en mert áb-en.'

"In answering chant they say, 'This is a good day, come out on to the land,' 'the north wind has come out,' 'the sky is doing according to our heart,' 'let us work and bind firm (?) our heart.'"

There are two kinds of corn—one tall with beards (barley?), the second shorter and not bearded; and the stalks of the reaped portion seem to be shown also.

A woman and a child are gleaning behind the reapers, the former with a heavy load on her back; another is cleverly carrying a basket and two vessels with provisions. One of them exclaims—

ámem nȧ nát fot, rack á-en em meshern ; em ȧr na en kehesu en sef, ḥer em pu hern

"Give me a hand (or a handful?); behold we shall come in the evening, do not repeat the meanness (?) of yesterday, cease it (?) to-day."

The comfort of the reapers is not forgotten: a light and artistically constructed shelter is

[1] Literally, "you old fellow, refuse of labourers," but there is a play upon the words *as* "hasten," and *as* "refuse."

seen on the right, beneath which are placed jars of wine or water; these have rounded bases, and some are supported on ring-stands of pottery, others on wooden frames. Several jars are outside, and an attendant holding a napkin and a large palm-leaf fan stands by, endeavouring to cool them with a current of air, ready for the monarch's arrival.

In the top row we see the short-stalked ears of corn taken in immense baskets to the threshing-floor. The baskets consist of net-work stretched on a frame, and are borne on a pole between two men. An overseer holding a twig in his hand calls out to the carriers—

ȧs-ten, meḥ refui-ten, pu mu áu, peḥ-ef na en qenáu

"Hasten yo, quicken your feet: the water is coming, and (will soon) reach the baskets." The inundation is coming before the harvest operations are complete.

The carriers say—

áu pa Shu shemu, te-tu en pa Shu suut át em remu

"The sun is hot, may the sun be given fish in payment for the corn." (The inundation would bring the fish.)

A man carrying back the pole of an empty basket, exclaims—

en uȧḥ pa nebá ḥer remen-á refui? su áb-á

"Haven't I stuck to the pole all day like a man? That is what I like!" (Lit. "Does not the pole stay-all-day on my shoulder very firmly? That is my wish.")

The corn on the threshing-floor forms a circular heap, high at the circumference and with a depression in the middle, in which the oxen are treading it out; a boy with a branch of a tree or broom of twigs sweeps in the strayed stalks. The oxen are five in number, not muzzled,[2] and are driven by a man with a whip, singing—

[2] Cf. Deuteronomy, ch. xxv., v. 4.

he-ten en-ten (sep sena), ahu, he-ten en-ten, he-ten en-ten; teḥa er am, at en nebn-ten; em refo erf en āb-ten: tutu qeb

"Thresh for yourselves, thresh for yourselves, oxen; thresh for yourselves, thresh for yourselves; straw to eat, corn for your masters; let not your hearts be still: it is cool."

The next process to which the corn is subjected is the winnowing, which is accomplished by tossing the threshed grain into the air with pairs of shovels shaped something like the sole of a foot. The operators wear cloths over their hair to protect it from the chaff; one of them is sweeping the grain together for the others to scoop up.

After this the results of the crops are measured: "the scribe of the accounts of corn, Tchuti-nefer" is registering, seated on a heap of corn, from which two labourers fill their measures, afterwards to empty them upon a second heap. Another labourer stands by, holding a shovel; probably he is noting the numbers upon his shovel, as a second scribe is generally figured in these scenes.

Finally sacks are filled at the second heap, conveyed to the walled granary, and there emptied. Of the granary we are shown the plan of the square enclosure and an elevation of the doorway at one corner, and the crenellated ornament at the top of the wall is indicated. It contains a tree (sycamore?) and four heaps of grain. The material composing one of them is quite unlike the grain in the other three, and possibly represents the flax-seed.

When the granary is full, the shipment of the supply due to the government granaries is next attended to, in the fourth row. Three boats are here seen just starting on their northward voyage, with the masts shipped and resting on the rudder-post, the pilots in the bows holding their sounding-poles, and a man drawing water; the grain-compartments are doubtless full. The rudder in all the boats is a broad oar turned in a rope bearing by means of a short lever. Close by are four other boats taking in cargo: the stepped (?) gangways are put to shore, and the labourers are emptying their sacks of corn into the barges. The inscription above reads:—

atep usekhu em at beteti: zef-sen ' en au ureḥ-n her fat at henā beteti ḥrzt: shenut meḥ, her nemesnies āḥāu en re-sen, ma usekhu atep tens, at her sef er heru: kher tutu her as-en em shent, as ḥati-en en khenut'

"Loading barges with wheat and barley; they say, 'Are we to spend the whole day carrying wheat and white barley?' The granaries are full, and heaps are pouring over their edges, the barges are heavy laden, and corn is jutting out: but the master is hastening us in going, behold our breasts are of bronze! (*i.e.* never fear, we are made of iron!).'"

Above, on the right, is Paheri "proceeding to load the barges." His words, translated above,[1] might perhaps be interpreted to apply only to the field-labourers who are putting in the cargo.

It will be observed that an abundant crop is hinted at throughout this scene; the cheerful idea of wealth and abundance is naturally implied in all the pictures.

(2) Registration of Cattle.

On the lower part of the wall, at the left end, is a scene much smaller than the last. Paheri is seated on a stool, writing; before him is a box, and above it on a tray the palette, a roll of papyrus, and a water-skin.

ḥeseb tennt menument āu ḥā en Anyt, mer aḥt nu ā resi, meḥ āb meukḥ en neb-ef shaā em Per-Hether nefuryt er Nekheb ān Paheri

"Counting the numbers of the cattle by the ha-prince of Anyt, the superintendent of the corn-fields of the southern district, the excellent satisfier of the heart of his lord, beginning

---

[1] P. 13.

from Per-Hathor[1] and reaching to Nekheb, the scribe Paheri."

The animals are driven towards him by their herds in four rows—oxen and cows with their calves in the upper two, and below asses, goats with kids, and swine. The asses are driven by a man with a whip, carrying a staff and a foot-hobble over his shoulder. The oxen lying bound upon the ground in the upper register are waiting to be branded; unfortunately the scene is imperfect, but one man appears to be heating the branding instrument at the fire, and another to be operating on an animal. The representation of swine is very rare.

Paheri's assistant in counting the animals is—

sen-ef mery-ef án áqer en un maá, se-kem nes, áqer nezu [-re?] Paheri maá kheru

"his brother, whom he loves, an excellent scribe of very truth, perfect in tongue, excellent in conversation, Paheri, deceased."[2] He receives the asses in the two lower rows, and a similar individual is seen in the two upper rows, in one case with traces of the same name, which has here been almost entirely erased.

(3) Receipt of Gold.

This scene is of the same extent as the last, except that the corn-ships have been intruded into one corner. Paheri is seated, holding staff and baton: he wears a peculiar head-covering, that falls down the back almost to the waist, and a collar (*usekh*) is on his breast. It is unfortunate that the inscription is mutilated in an important passage, leaving the sense doubtful—

shesep neb en ḥeru qeru .... en shesep shayt em á kherpu un temá pen, án res tep shu em beḳi, tem meh[a ḥer] tetet em ḥer(i)-ef ḥá Paheri

"Receiving the gold of the chief miners.........

.... receiving what has been ordained from the superintendents of this town, by the prince Paheri, watchful without tiring, not failing in what has been entrusted to him."

His brother Paheri again assists, recording the amounts. In the upper row four contributors are looking on in a respectful attitude, while the gold rings are weighed in the scales against an ox-shaped weight; another man, kneeling, watches the tongue of the balance, and perhaps the plummet;[2] above are the rings in four heaps. In the lower row three bags of ore or dust are seen, beside rings; a box and a tray are in front of Paheri's brother, the scribe Paheri II., and apparently one of the four men above is having a taste of the stick, his contribution not being sufficient. The names of two of the others are given, viz., *her mert Menu* (?) and *her mert Heru*, the chiefs of serfs Menu (?) and Heru.

The inscriptions in the temple of Redesiyeh show that there were certain gold workings in the Eastern desert the produce of which would reach the Nile valley not far from El Kab.

On the river are two ships passing each other; one is going south, with sail up, the other, with mast shipped, is being rowed northward down the stream. The latter is probably bound for Thebes, while the former is just arriving thence for a cargo of bullion. The two ships are exactly alike, each having a deck-house with two windows and look-out platform at bow and stern. A chariot is on the top of the deck-house, and the horses are in the bows behind the pilot; all this, with the painted decoration fore and aft, shows that they are not mere vessels of burthen, but are fitted up for the nomarch's voyages. At the bows of the vessel sailing southward is a pilot with a sounding-pole to try the depth and avoid the shallows; over him is written—

---

[1] Denderah, see above, p. 6.
[2] For this Paheri II., see p. 8.

[3] For the action, see Petrie, *Season in Egypt*, pl. xx., and p. 42.

ury-en mu menu er Per neh, (emt uezca shut
"Let us give the signal (or sing the chorus?), come and moor at Per-mb (the house of gold), a city pleasant of *shut* (glitter or shadow?)."
The steersman replies—

em shu em kheru-ek, pu eati em ta hat

"Do not *shu* (waste) thy voice (or, do not fail to speak), O thou who art in the bows!"
The alliteration of *shu* with *shut* is evidently the comic feature of this reply.

PAHERI'S UNOFFICIAL LIFE AND AMUSEMENTS.
Pl. iv.

On this section of the wall[1] we have a series of representations from the private and domestic life and affairs of Paheri. They may for convenience be grouped round the three large figures of the nomarch—(1) Paheri watching the fishermen and fowlers; (2) Paheri with his wife seated under an awning, receiving fruits; (3) Paheri, with the little prince Uaxmos upon his lap, receiving linen and ointments.

(1) Watching the Fishermen and Fowlers.

This scene occupies the lower third of the plates: Paheri leans on his staff, and watches—

ma sekhet apfu, ham remu, sr-zu her em kat nebt arert em sekhet, in ha Paheri maa kheru

"seeing the netting of wild fowl, the capture of fish, rejoicing the countenance with all the works performed in the river-meadows, by the *ha*-prince Paheri, deceased."

In the lower row a clap-net has been laid in a pool between clumps of papyrus, and the wild fowl have settled over it.[2] An old man

---

[1] On the left side of the plate is seen the fissure in the rock. There has been no fresh injury to its right-hand edge, but on the left there have been two unsuccessful attempts to cut out groups, deep grooves having been chiselled out all round them.

[2] The water crowded with birds is faintly indicated in the original, but is not clear enough to reproduce.

---

on the watch behind the reeds gives the signal, and no less than nine men pull the rope which closes the net; the end of the rope has been secured round a post in the ground. We next see the captives plucked, trimmed with a knife on a sloping board, and put into jars for keeping. A crane is brought straight to Paheri.

In the upper row a large net with its floats is drawn ashore, full of fish; the catch is carried up to an old man, who splits each fish and lays it out to dry in the sun. We see also a veteran with a spindle making twine, with which the same or another manufactures the net. The attitudes of these two figures are characteristic of the processes. The one gives the spindle a twist on his thigh, the other grasps the end of the net between his toes.

(2) Paheri and his Wife seated under an Awning, receiving Fruits, &c.

This occupies the middle of the wall, and may be held to include a vintage scene and a group of the relatives of Paheri's wife.

At the top is a representation of the vintage. The vines are trellised, and the stems banked round at the roots with earth, which is cupped to hold the water and keep the ground moist. The grapes are gathered by men and women, put into baskets, and conveyed to the wine-press. At each end of the wine-press is fixed an upright forked pole, to support a bar laid across; the men treading the grapes in the trough steady themselves by grasping the ropes which hang from the middle of the cross-bar. Rows of amphorae are seen above, and a man who is no doubt filling them with a jar from the wine-press.

The products of the vineyard and gardens, as well as the fish and fowl from the nets, are offered to Paheri and his wife. They are seated together, with her arm round his neck, in an arbour. This arbour has a roof of rushes (coloured green), and a mat of the same is on the ground beneath their feet. Hcnut-er-nchch holds a lotus flower, and vegetables resembling the seed-vessels of the lotus as figured on the monuments. The inscription reads—

sekhemkh ah ma ha nefer, &c.

"Diverting the heart and seeing good fortune by the ha-prince of Nekheb, Paheri, deceased, and the mistress of a house, Henut-er-nehch." Strings of pomegranates, grapes, and the flowers, buds and leaves of the lotus, cucumbers in baskets, and a bottle, presumably full of fresh grape juice (as it figures in the vintage scene), are being brought to them by three men in one row. The bottle is of a very remarkable shape, and is evidently identical with a vessel found by Mr. Petrie at Gurob, which was formed of the egg of an ostrich furnished with a long wooden spout. In the second row we note especially the ducks, lotuses, and papyrus flowers from the marshes.

The relatives of Paheri's wife are looking on as guests, and sit facing the arbour. The principal figures are "his wife's father, the chief superintendent of gold miners, Ruru," "his wife's mother Ta-amey," and "her son, the officer of his majesty, Teta." These are seated side by side on chairs, and are attended by two women with vases of unguents and wine (?); one of the attendants, named Khnemt, is so good a musician that she is entitled "the musician of the goddess Nekhebt" *(qemáyt ent Nekhebt)*; between them is a large jar wreathed with a lotus, over the mouth a round platter (?). Behind the first three were probably eight more members of the family in two rows; several have been destroyed by the fracture of the rock, but we can trace or restore in the upper row—(1) "her son Se," (2) ...., (3) .... (son), (4) "her daughter Usert"; in the lower row—(1) "her daughter Henut-ta-mehu," (2) ....,

(3) .... (daughter), (4) "her daughter Henut-urt."[1]

(3) Paheri Dandling Prince Uazmes.

In the top register Paheri is seated, wearing a thin vest, loin cloth and tunic, with the royal child upon his lap. The latter is nude, with an amulet ☥ round his neck, and the princely lock of hair on the right side of the head.

sekhemkh ah em khet neht, art hru nefer, shesp nezt her, tuat Nehebkan, on men hi en sa-seten Uazmes ha Paheri maá kheru

"Rejoicing the heart with everything, making holiday, receiving gifts, worshipping Nehebkau, by the tutor of prince Uazmes, the ha-prince Paheri, deceased."

The figures and inscriptions beyond are now grievously mutilated, but a good deal can be learnt from the copies of Hay and Burton.[2] There were figures of adults and children bringing offerings in two rows, and the inscription indicates that some of them were Paheri's children. In the shrine (pl. x.) three sons and three daughters are represented, and as there is room for six adult figures in the two rows here, it might be thought that these exactly represented the children of Paheri; but there are four, if not five, women amongst them, so this is impossible. In the upper row we can recognize the names of Ta-khenemset, Ta-tetetes, and Nebt-taui, the three daughters of Paheri; the figures in the lower row must have been of friends or servants. The inscription over the upper row runs—

mesch nez-[her án mes]u-ef, mesu mesu-ef, tuat (?)...

"Bringing offerings by his children and grandchildren, adoring (?) ......" The figure of one little granddaughter remains; but her name, if it was written at all, is now lost.

[1] The restoration in the *Description de l'Égypte*, Ant. i., pl. 68, is evidently imaginary and incorrect.
[2] The complete restoration in the *Description de l'Égypte* is again quite wrong.

The inscription over the lower row (in which we can see that there was one man offering between two women) reads—

meseh [........] henket renpet neb, tuat (?) *upt renpet* "Bringing .. .. and offerings and all kinds of flowers, adoring (? or 'on the morning of'?) the New Year.'"

FUNERARY SCENES. Pl. v.

At the inner end of the West wall is a representation of the ceremonies, real or imaginary, which might take place at the funeral of Paheri. Scenes of the same character are found in several contemporary tombs at Thebes; but those hitherto published, while they throw a great deal of light on the subject, are insufficient to enable one to construct a clear statement of the order of events, or to explain many of the strange objects and figures that are met with in them. The ceremonies are represented with great elaboration in the magnificent tomb of Rekhmara at Thebes, dating from the end of the long reign of Thothmes III. and the beginning of that of Amenhotep II., and we have referred constantly to the valuable plates of M. Virey's memoir on that tomb[2] in drawing up the following description; but the variation in detail and arrangement is very great. The ceremonies provided an immense series of subjects to select from, so that probably no two tombs would show all the same. The artist of Paheri's tomb was compelled by want of space to restrict his selection within very moderate bounds. Professor Maspero has pointed out in a similar case that an inscription explaining a scene which the artist has thought good to omit has been wrongly retained, and does duty for a totally different subject. This is possibly the explanation of some apparently inappropriate legends which the reader may observe in the present instance.

It may be that all the scenes refer to one long-drawn ceremony, namely, the presentation of the mummy to various divinities and temples, accompanied by symbolical acts and offerings.

The hawk in the middle of the scene has been cut out recently, a large circular patch being defaced in the process. The restoration in the plate is from the copies of Burton, Hay and Rosellini.

a. In the top row we see the funeral sledge drawn in procession by men and oxen.[3] The rope is attached to a bar fixed upon the horns of the cattle, which are urged on with whip and gesture by the driver. Four men are hauling at the rope, three are chanting (?) with raised arms, one is burning incense; and there is one group erased. In the parallel scenes of the tomb of Rekhmara these men are styled *reth, puit, rekhyt uebt,* which means, perhaps, "people in general—both the present and past generations," all of whom do honour to the deceased. The erasure of a group is noticeable there also.

The sledge is covered by a canopy, beneath which the mummy rests upon an ornamented bier, which itself is placed upon a box or coffin. At the head is the female *tert shert,* "younger mourner," representing Nephthys, and at the foot the *tert dat,* "older mourner," for Isis.

The inscription over the procession reads—

árt qrest nefert en hà Paheri, s-árt hà Paheri muá kheru er áis-f en Kher-neter, em hetep, em hetep kher neter áu. Uza em hetep er úakhet, er Sekhet Áaru, er tuat ; er semt er bu enti hà Paheri pen àm

---

[1] It was customary on New Year's Day for an estate or household to offer gifts to the master.

[2] *Mémoires publiés par la Mission Archéologique Française au Caire,* tome v., 1er fascicule, *Le tombeau de Rekhmara,* par Ph. Virey. The grouping of the funeral scenes is shown on pl. xix., and the details on the succeeding plates.

[3] Compare *Rekhmara,* pl. xxi., bottom row.

"Making a good burial for the prince Paheri, conveying the Prince Paheri justified to his chamber of the Kherneter, in peace, in peace before the great god. Proceeding in peace to the horizon, to the Field of Reeds, to the Tuat: to lead to (any) place where this prince Paheri (may be)."

b. Behind the "chief mourner" is *kher heb her tep*, "the chief lector," holding a scroll.[1] The vertical line of inscription reads—

met âu kher heb her tep, "*em hetep, em hetep kher neter âu*"

"Said by the chief lector, 'In peace, in peace, before the great god.'" Two other persons with larger wigs and long staves close the procession; they are evidently people of some distinction. In order to preserve the clear representation in profile, and avoid a back view, the artist has chosen to put their staves in the advanced left hands, instead of in the right. The inscription runs—

met âu shesu "*uza em hetep, em hetep, er âs-f en kher-neter; shesep fu emem uru (âau ?) em shes en neter âu*"

"Said by the followers (of the procession), 'Proceed in peace, in peace to his (sic) chamber of Kher-neter (the necropolis); receive banquets among the nobles (or the aged ones?) as a follower of the great god.'"

c. In the second row the priest (the "officiating priest" in Rekhmara[2]), with a tall censor (*âr seneter* "censing"), precedes four persons (who are the *semeru* "friends" in Rekhmara) bearing a chest supported by poles on their shoulders; between the bearers are visible the two mourners, with their arms in a characteristic attitude.

d. A group of two men dancing, *kheb mau* "dancing of the buffoons;[3] four shrines—one between two palm trees, over two rectangular spaces, the first enclosing two pools (?), the second being a doorway (?). In Rekhmara this seems to represent the arrival at the temple at Pe (Buto). An officiating priest holding an enormous scroll greets a boat on its arrival—

zet âu kher heb em hetep em hetep kher neter âu

"Said by the officiating priest, 'In peace, in peace before the great god.'" The boat is towed by a *semer* "friend," *sem*-priest, and an *âm khent*: it contains a tall chest, against which the two mourners, *tert âat* and *tert shert*, have seated themselves, closely wrapped. The same or another officiating priest, holding a scroll and raising his arm in declamation, appears behind the boat, by the side of an upright structure, crowned with *kheker* ornament ☥. Over the boat is the inscription—

Seht hâ Paheri em ta heqt âh aptu em âbt usekht. Met âu kher-heb ârt-nef temâ em .... neter en Ânpu em âbt usekht âu hâ Paheri maâ kheru

"Entertaining (?) the prince Paheri with bread, beer, flesh and fowl in (?) the Hall. Said by the officiating priest, 'The prince Paheri, deceased, has made for himself a mansion in the temple of Anubis and in (?) the Hall.'"

c. Two men holding long papyrus stalks precede a sledge drawn by three others. Upon the sledge is a somewhat shapeless mass, of which more below. The inscription, preserved by Hay and Rosellini, reads—

er Âmentet, er Âmentet, pa ta netem ânkh, er bu en nuen-ek âm-ef yh âu me-ki âu (The last lines are identical in the two copies.)

"To the West, to the West, the land pleasant for life, to the place in which thou art (?): lo! come, behold I (?) come."

The object upon the sledge is of considerable interest, for it seems to be the victim for a human sacrifice, enclosed in the skin of an ox. A very similar object laid upon a table, and with a human head and hand projecting from it, is figured in the corresponding scenes

---

[1] Cf. *Rekhmara*. pl. xxiii., middle row, for this scene.
[2] *I.e.*, same row as last.
[3] *I.e.*, pl. xx., xxi., top row.

SCENES AND INSCRIPTIONS.

of the tomb of Rekhmara at Thebes,[1] and is there called Teknu; but the connection with human sacrifice is derived from the scenes of the tomb of Montuherkhepeshef, excellently interpreted by Professor Maspero.[2] In this the Teknu is on the sledge, as in our tomb, crouching, while the hide is carried in front of the sledge;[3] and he is afterwards[4] included in the contents of a pit, apparently a fire-pit, in which a number of objects were consumed. A real, or perhaps fictitious, human sacrifice is pretty clearly indicated in another of the paintings in the same tomb:[5] the Theban necropolis requires diligent searching for further evidence of the practice. Professor Maspero states that a statue of the deceased is sometimes represented in the sledge-scene in place of the Teknu: if this is certainly a statue of the deceased, and not a figure substituted for the living Teknu, it follows that the Teknu may have been a victim to represent the owner of the tomb in some ceremony of consecrating the tomb *before* the final interment.

The statement of Plutarch,[6] that human burnt sacrifices were offered at Eileithyia (Nekheb), is perhaps no more than a very remarkable coincidence.

f. The tall chest is in a boat upon the water, with a large censer burning upon a stand in front of it.[7] One of the female mourners is kneeling in the prow, and in the stern a man stands holding a paddle. The boat appears to be already alongside the bank, for another figure is kneeling outside the boat, holding the same paddle; the artist has, however, represented the last as if he were kneeling in the water. The prow of the boat touches the symbol of the Kher-neter, represented by a mount, in which is fixed a lofty perch with a hawk on the top, while the sign 𓈋 is at the foot.

g. A figure, apparently Paheri himself, is kneeling before the shrine and image of Anubis, represented as a jackal upon a pylon.[8] Paheri's sarcophagus is in a boat behind him, placed upon a bier, with the mourners at the head and foot, while three men are about to remove the lid (?), or to carry the sarcophagus in their arms. The latter action is perhaps indicated in the tomb of Rekhmara. The inscription is—

spee ee Anpu khent   neteʾ e, ḥe ee tu er Abḥu ān
    ḥā Paheri

"Approaching to Anubis in the shrine, landing at Abydos by the prince Paheri." The first part of this inscription relates to the above scene, but the second is applicable only to the ceremonies in the next row.

h. The lower row is closed by a large seated figure of Osiris in a shrine, holding the crook and flail:[9] the god is mummified, and wears the crown of Upper Egypt. He is entitled—

Āsir khent Āmentiu, neter āa, ḥeqa zet

"Osiris khent-Amenti, great god, ruler of eternity."

Before him are two stands with lotus flowers and two trays piled with offerings, which consist of joints of meat, a goose, a cucumber, cakes, &c. This offering is made by Paheri, who, having removed his wig and tunic, kneels in the simplest costume, and raises his arms to the deity—

ḥā en Nekheb Paheri mau kheru zet-ef: 'auez her-ek neter pen shepsi, neb ta, ur Abez (?) āa em Abḥu: in-uri kher-ek neb-ri em ḥetep, ḥetep-ek uā; ān uek ḥetepu, seṭem-ek nas-ā ār-ek zefet-ā, nuk uā em fuauu tu'

---

[1] Cf. *Rekhmara*, pl. xxvi.
[2] *Mémoires de la Miss. Arch. Franç.*, tome v., fasc. 3, p. 435 ff.
[3] *L.c.*, p. 439.
[4] *L.c.*, p. 457.
[5] *L.c.*, p. 452. Two non-Egyptians are being strangled.
[6] *De Iside et Osiride*, cap. 73.
[7] Cf. *Rekhmara*, pl. xxvi., top row.

[8] *L.c.*, pl. xxiv., middle row.
[9] *L.c.*, pl. xxvii.

"The prince of Nekheb Paheri, deceased, he says, 'Hail to thee, O (this) noble god, lord of earth, great of the nome of This, mighty in Abydos: I have come to thee, my lord, in peace, give me peace: there are for thee peace-offerings, hear thou my call, do thou my words: I am one of those that adore thee.'"

Behind this the scenes are again on the smaller scale, in two half-rows.

i. In the upper half-row is a sledge, closely resembling that in the top row, and containing a tall chest or coffin upon a bier, and covered with a canopy. Two men, preceded by an officiating priest holding a scroll, draw it towards—

j. Three palms and two bushy trees over a tank of water, with a small rectangular garden plot (?) above, divided into eight squares for irrigation;[1] on the edge of the plot are placed six ring-stands (?) for jars of water. This figure is puzzling: Mr. Tylor would explain it as a draught-board with the pieces for play on the edge.

k. The remainder of the half-row is occupied by ten shrines: three of them are open, disclosing the deities, one of whom is jackal-headed, the other two human-headed. In the tomb of Rekhmara[2] the shrines are fourteen in number, and the inscriptions show that they belonged to very various deities, mostly obscure, but including the four sons of Horus—Amset, Hapi, Tuamotef, and Qebh-senuf—who are well known in funerary scenes.

In the lower half-row is, first—

l. A structure resembling a gateway, with what may be the rectangular plan of the building to which it gave entrance laid out flat above. In the gateway are two buffoons wearing tall caps formed of reeds tied in a bunch at the top. These buffoons are named *muu* in the tomb of Rekhmara.[3]

m. The two mourners, the elder *ert dat* and behind her the younger *ert shert*, are offering bowls of liquid before four libation-tables (?) or pools of water (?). The scene in the tomb of Rekhmara[4] represents these like pools full of water, and the mourners are there designated by other titles, *semtet* and *kenut*, the last possibly meaning "gardener."

n. Behind the mourners is a second shrine of Osiris facing the first (*h*). The figure, *Asir neter āa*, "Osiris, the great god," is represented in the same way as in the larger shrine, but standing instead of sitting.

o. Behind the shrine is a rectangular enclosure, ornamented or hedged in with the *kheker* ⟨ usually found on the tops of high outer walls or as an ornament for the cornice of roofed chambers; within it stand four human figures without visible arms. In the tomb of Rekhmara[5] the legend with these figures seems to read, *netera, āvin dan uru*, "Gods, keepers of the great gates."

4. EAST WALL. Pl. VI.-VIII.

The scenes here are only two in number, and seem from their subject to complete the domestic scenes of the central part of the West wall. They are on a large scale, and are probably enacted within doors, as opposed to the out-door scenes on the opposite wall. The first is a great banquet, of which numerous ancestors, relatives, and friends partake, and to which a formal and probably a funereal character is given by the presence of a robed priest to perform an opening ceremony; the second is an act of worship to the gods, accompanied by an inscription which, as summarizing the scenes in the tomb, may be taken for the starting-point or the finishing-point of all the

---

[1] Cf. *Rekhmara*, pl. xxvii.
[2] *L.c.*, pl. xxvi., top row, and pl. xxviii.
[3] *L.c.*, pl. xxvi., top row.

[4] *L.c.*, pl. xxvii.
[5] *L.c.*, pl. xxiv., top row.

sculptures. The portions recently damaged have been restored in the plates from the copies of Hay and Burton.

THE BANQUET. Pl. vi., vii.

The principal personages are (1) Paheri and his wife, whose figures are fully life-size; they are seated at a separate table, and their son Amenmes performs before them a ceremony of offering that is probably confined to banquets to the dead. (2) Paheri's father Atefrura, and his wife Kem, and Paheri's maternal grandfather, Aahmes son of Abana, and his wife Apu; these are seated at two tables and are on a medium scale. The rest of the figures are smaller, in four rows, the men in the upper rows separate from the women in the lower; these subordinate personages, maternal relatives and friends, ranging from the great-aunt of Paheri to his brothers and sisters, are seated on mats and are waited on by male and female servants, while a band of musicians entertains the party. Excepting the principal personages, the guests all wear on their heads the peculiar conical objects usually associated with such representations. The name is written over each, and in the case of the women some imaginary conversations are recorded, which, like those on the opposite wall, are instructive if not amusing. Lotus buds or flowers are in the hands of nearly all; the women invariably have one tied round the head-dress.

To proceed to the details. The decorated border on the left is composed of oblong panels of blue, red, yellow, and green alternately, separated from each other by a bar of white between two of black; the whole enclosed between two green lines which run from top to bottom of the scene.

The large figure of Paheri[1] wears a full-bottomed wig, a broad collar, and bracelets.

The body is made to the waist, his dress consisting of the loin-cloth and long transparent skirt, and he holds a napkin in his right hand while the left is stretched out to the offerings. Henut-er-neheh has the usual tight-fitting dress suspended from the left shoulder; the chest and arms are bare excepting that she wears a broad collar and bracelets: anklets are also visible below the dress; on her head is the usual covering, which falls over the shoulders: it is tied round with a fillet of rosettes, having a lotus flower between two buds on the forehead. A tame baboon, coloured grey, is tied to the back leg of the chair on which these two are seated; the animal is helping himself from a basket of fruit, perhaps sycamore figs. The inscription above is—

hā mer hā nā neter en Nekhbt, meh ab meukh en neb-ef, ān Paheri māā kheru: hemt-ef maret-ef ent est āb-ef nebt per Henut-er-neheh māāt kheru

"The ha-prince, superintendent of the priests of the goddess Nekhebt, excellent satisfier of the heart of his lord, the scribe Paheri deceased: his wife whom he loves of the place of his heart, the lady of a house Henut-er-neheh deceased." In front of the figures was a table of offerings, which has been neatly cut out by the excavators of the later chambers; the lotus flowers which lay on the top of the offerings alone remain. Above are the names of the offerings in a rectangle spaced for twenty-two in two rows; amongst them are *mu*, "water," *ārp*, "wine," *bāt*, "honey," with cakes of various sorts, flesh and fowl. The "determinatives" indicating the nature of each named offering are below the names, and numerals for the quantities (whether one or two of each) are put in separate lines. Amenmes, a favourite son of Paheri, who appears also in the scene of worship,[2] officiates, wearing the leopard skin, as was the custom in important ceremonies of offering. The skin is fastened on the shoulder

---

[1] Pl. vi. [2] Pl. viii.

in a peculiar way; besides the skin, Amenmes wears only a loin-cloth, bracelets, and a broad collar. His inscription, partly cut away in front below, can be restored—

[irt fr setcu hetep ou sa-ef] mer-ef, Amen-mes, ze f-ef ' en ka-ten, per kheru em khet nebt, àu nàb '

" Performance of the (ceremony) to setcu hetep by his son whom he loves, Amenmes; he says, 'For your ka-s, a funereal offering of every kind of thing: it is pure.'" This formula is generally supposed to have been used only in offerings to the dead, but conceivably it may be a kind of " grace before meals," to be repeated at any banquet. In front of the sitting figures are the words sma er khet nebt nefert nàbt, "partaking of all good and pure things."

Below this was a row of serfs bringing animals, etc., for the banquet. The cutting of the door has removed most of them, but two remain, with a goat, a gazelle, and a hare. Beyond the door they are received by the scribe Paheri II., who notes their contributions upon a tablet or papyrus. His inscription must be restored somewhat thus—

shesep [nect her] àu sen-ef mery-ef en est ab-ef àu àger en tep-heseb Paheri maà kheru kher neter àa

"Receiving offerings by his brother whom he loves, of the place of his heart, the excellent scribe of accounts, Paheri, justified before the great god."

This brother of Paheri reappears on the West wall[1] with the same name and epithets. Four small figures hold the baggage for the scribe.[2] The shesu Ar-hât-sen "attendant Ar-hat-sen" carries a roll of papyrus in his hand, and strapped to his back a large object, which may be a water-skin in a frame, with long flexible neck; the attendant Teta carries the sandals and a bag(?) over his shoulder; the "attendant whom he loves of the place of his heart" (shesu

mer-ef en est àb-ef) named Kha, carries the staff and stool, while the seh (?) mer-ef en est àb-ef, "neighbour(?) whom he loves of the place of his heart Aputa," bears two bags and brings up the rear.

As Paheri and his wife look down the tomb, the rest of the participators in the banquet are seated facing them.[3] First we have the ancestors at their two tables. The upper group is the famous "chief of sailors, Aahmes, son of Abana," with "his wife, the lady of a house, Apu"—

(her khenyt Aahmes sa A-bana, hemt-ef nebt per A-pu)

An animal resembling a greyhound is tied to their chair; it has been much defaced. The lower group is Atefrura, tutor of the king's son Uazmes, and his wife Kem. We know from his own tomb that Aahmes, son of Abana, was Paheri's maternal grandfather, and from this tomb that Atefrura was his father.

The lesser personages are dressed much like the ancestors, but have no anklets or armlets. The relationships indicated by the inscriptions are generally with Paheri himself, "his brother," "his grandmother's sister's son," &c.; but in the two lower rows "her son," "her daughter," &c., refer to the son or daughter of Kem, who, as we have said already, was Paheri's mother.

In the top row Paheri's brother Herari "receives all good things and makes holiday" (shesep khet nebt nefert, àrt hru nefer àn, &c.); he is smelling a lotus flower, and a servant, nba en pa hà Pa-behet, "the butler of the ha-prince, Pa-behet," offers him a bowl of liquid, while he holds two tiny jug-like vases in his left hand. The bowl is evidently of embossed metal, from the character of the ornament upon it.

Behind Herari sits Paheri's second cousin Teta (sa en sent ent met ent met-ef, lit. "son of the sister of the mother of his mother"), who

---

[1] Pl. iii.   [2] Cf. pl. iii., left-hand end.   [3] Pl. vii.

was an "attendant of His Majesty." Next is his cousin Mezay-se, of the same degree, and then "his mother's brother" Mey: the last appears to refuse the proffered bowl, and the servant, who holds a deep jar, empty, in his left hand, says, *at-nà nekt, nah-à tu*, "Command me something, and I will let thee alone." The servants of Paheri are evidently very importunate in their attentions to the visitors, as they should be in the house of so generous a host.

The next name is much erased; we can, however, discern *khenems-ef*......... *Tetà*, "his friend A-hotep, son of (?) Teta;" next "his friend the *kher-heb* Tehuti-mes," and, last in the row, "his mother's brother Meshau."

The second row shows us Paheri's brothers— (1) Aahmes; (2) Paman, "an attendant of his majesty"; (3) Sen-mes, a "guardian of Amen"; (4) Tehuti-em-hat; (5) Amen-hotep, an "officer of his majesty"; also, a "friend" with the inscription erased, and his second cousin Kem. The servant who offers a jar to Tehuti-em-hat is "the butler Teta."

We next come to the female relatives.

In the third row are three daughters of Kem, viz. [Thu]pu, Nub-em-heb, and Amen-sat; also Paheri's second cousin Nub-mehy, and his three nurses,[1] Hepu (*mendt-ef Hepu*), Sensenbet, and Thupu. Amensat refuses the bowl, and the servant says jestingly—

u ka-et s-urà er tekkt, ur kru nefer, a setem na zet tayt art, em ur feht em àzau (?)

"For thy *ka*, drink to drunkenness, make holiday; O listen to what thy companion is saying, do not weary of taking (?)."

Her companion and distant cousin Nub-mehy is saying to the servant, "Give me eighteen cups of wine, behold I should love (to drink) to drunkenness, my inside is as dry as straw!"—

ǎmensat-em XVIII en yerà en urp, mek uer en er tekkt, ast aua-à en heha (lit. "the place in me is of straw").

Another servant addresses Sensenbet. "He says, 'Drink, do not refuse (?); behold I am not going to leave you'"—

zet-ef suri, em ar ar zeb; mest àen àuau er nub-et

And Thupu seconds his efforts: "Drink, do not spoil the entertainment: and let the cup come to me: behold it is due to the *ka* to drink"—

suri em ar hua theuf, fes-t puh-uu àa sethet: mest uesi pu hà en suau

The tone of conversation at these parties is not higher than one would expect from the representations of convivial scenes which Wilkinson copied at Thebes.

In the bottom row are the musicians. The harpist wears an ostrich feather in her hair, which is dressed like that of a man; in front of her is a young girl with clappers, dancing; a woman playing on the double pipe; and three women seated, clapping their hands to mark time.

Behind the musicians are Amen-Sat and Tetuta, great-aunts of Paheri; the latter is accompanied by her daughters Zab, Ty, and Nub-em-nehebt.

PAHERI WORSHIPPING. Pl. viii.

Paheri, represented on a large scale, upholds in each hand a censer with five wicks; behind him stands his wife and three of their children, the latter on a small scale: they are *sat-ef urt mert-ef Ta-tet-ers*, "his eldest daughter, whom he loves, Tatetes"; *sa-ef mer-ef Amenmes*, "his son, whom he loves, Amenmes"; and "his son Ra-hotep." The first two appear to have been the eldest *surviving* children; the order of the names in the shrine[2] indicates that they were born after Takhenemset and Khu-em-uast.

---

[1] *Khenems* "honoured friend," and *menàt* "nurse," would almost seem to be used as parallel honorific terms for male and female acquaintances, respectively.

[2] Pl. x.

The inscription in large characters before Paheri reads—

*hetep em set amentet, pert em ba er ma uten; un
uart en ankh aqer em kher-neter; efet-nef shemt-
f, aq pert em ba ankhy, ert hekenu en .Im tuat,
ata khet neht neferi nabt en Ra Hru-aakhti en
Nekhebt neht pet, en Hat-her hert tept set, en Usir
neter aa, en Anpu neb ta zeser; te-sen se-sent nef
nezem en mehyt; ua, &c.*

" Repose in the Western mountain, coming forth upon the land to see the sun's disk, opening of the roads to the perfect spirit who is in Kher-neter; may he be allowed to walk out, to enter and go forth as a living soul; to give offerings to Him who is in the other world (Osiris), and to present all good and pure things to Ra-Horus of the two horizons, to Nekhebt lady of heaven, to Hathor princess of the mountain, to Osiris the great god, and to Anubis lord of the sacred land; that they may give the breathing of the pleasant breeze of the north wind; by " the ha-prince Paheri and his wife.

This is apparently a summing-up of all the scenes in the tomb : Paheri's desire for future life was to have access both to the world of the dead and the world of the living, and in the latter he would wish to enjoy again the times of prosperity which he had passed through on earth: it was for this reason that he caused them to be represented in the paintings.

Beyond the hieroglyphs are four piles of offerings on reed mats. The top row consists evidently of jars containing the seven sacred oils, so often represented; in the next is a gorgeously coloured goose, with the haunch of an animal, a wooden stand with offerings, &c. In the third heap is a bunch of onions, and three jars of liquids, placed on ring-stands, are wreathed with lotuses.

Behind the offerings four female musicians are standing, holding up in their right hands the sacred rattle 𓏞 called by the classical writers *sistrum*; another instrument, the *menāt*, formed partly of a string of beads of various hues, hangs down in their left hands. In the third row is a male figure, much injured, holding a branch of lotuses in the right hand and a vase (?) in the left. The signs over his head seem to indicate that he is the "[priest of] the goddess Nekhebt, Sen......"

Beneath this scene four men are bringing offerings to the banquet, or to the sacrifice above.[1] The leader of these has a very large bunch of flower-stems (*sa en sent ant met ent hemt-ef* .... *Kem* (?) " .... Kem (?) the son of the sister of the mother of his wife," in other words Paheri's uncle by marriage); next, bearing a jar of wine (?) and a live goose is *kauti Sen-nefer*, "the gardener Sen-nefer"; and after him "the gardener Uhemu," with white cakes (coloured white) and lotus flowers. Behind these are butchers cutting up two oxen and conveying the joints to the same destination as the others. The *seten* (?) ("butcher") Then-na is endeavouring, with the help of an assistant, to separate the foreleg from the carcase of one of the animals; one man is taking some ribs, another a foreleg.

At the south end of the wall is a border of coloured rectangles, similar to that at the northern end, described on p. 23.

5. LONGITUDINAL INSCRIPTIONS (FRIEZE AND CEILING).

THE line of large hieroglyphs over the scenes on the West wall, from end to end of the main chamber,[2] reads—

[u hetep seten Usir khent Amentiu, neteru āmu Kher-neter, te-sen se-sent nef nezem en meht, irt kheperu em ba ankh, en ka en Usir ha Paheri maā kheru. Un-ek pequ em shert kemt, te-tu uek met em Ta-uent, ām-ek shnas, suri-ek mehā her khat ent neter aā, ful-ek em peru khentui: an hetept-ek em Ankh-

---

[1] Compare pl. vi.   [2] Pl. iii.-v., top.

tani; sekhem-ek em mu er hetep abeh, ses-u-ek uf en uaht, amakhy kher Aupu Usr ha Paheri maā kheru

"A royal offering (?) give Osiris Khent-Amentiu, and the gods who are in Kher-neter, may they give the smelling of the sweet breeze of the north wind, and the making of transformations as a living soul, to the ghost of the Osiris, the *ha*-prince Paheri, deceased. Mayest thou bite the cakes of black barley (?), may there be given to thee a staff in Tanent, mayest thou eat a loaf, and drink a cup of milk on the altar of the great god, and mayest thou receive gifts in the inner houses: may there be offerings for thee in Ankh-taui, mayest thou have water at command to thy heart's desire: mayest thou breathe the breeze of the north wind, O trusty before Anubis, Osiris, *ha*-prince Paheri, deceased!"

Similarly on the opposite side:—

seten hetep te Nekhebt hezt Nekhen, fat-u(?) uekh Fak²(?); Het-her herb tept set; Osir hug zet; Aupu khent .... neter em ul, Neb Ta-zeser, Set Amentet, aäht khet, anqet qesu, se-ment säh er cat-ef: tesen per-kheru ta heqt äbu apta kebs (?) sesneter merhet hetept zefa khet nebt nefert näht henket am en netar, hau [her?³] khet em tep tran, peçert her vth en câ neb; as ka en hā en Nekheb ha Paheri maā kheru; zef-ef 'a tetpu ta heqt en han menkhu em per Usir, to-ten ta heqt er terni en ha henā-ten, āmakhy kher Usar ha en Nekheb Paheri, maā kheru'

"A royal offering give Nekhebt, the white one of Nekhen, wide-stretching (with wings), mistress of Fak; and Hathor, princess of the desert: and Osiris, king of eternity: and Anubis in the shrine, who is in the Oasis (?), lord of Ta-zeser: and the Western desert which offers (?) the corpse, embraces the bones, and lays the noble mummy in its place; that they may give funerary meals, bread, beer, oxen, wild-fowl, linen, incense, wax, offerings, foods, and all good and pure things of which offerings are made to a deity, beyond the offerings at the beginnings of the seasons, and what appears upon the altar daily; to the *ka* of the *ha*-prince of Nekheb, the scribe Paheri, deceased; he says, 'O ye who give bread and beer to the excellent souls in the house of Osiris, give ye bread and beer twice daily (?) to the soul who is with you, the devout before Osiris, the *ha*-prince of Nekheb, Paheri, deceased.'"

The middle line on the ceiling and the two side lines above the khaker ornament are too much mutilated to be readily copied.

---

6. THE BACK WALL AND NICHE.
Pl. IX.-X.

The Back Wall. Pl. ix.

The inscription on the Back wall is remarkable for its length; the themes are the usual ones—the virtues of the deceased, the prayers for a happy future, and the desire that visitors should repeat formulae to ensure ample food for the ghost. The ha-prince of Nekheb was a careful man, who knew the value of detail; he was an "excellent scribe of accounts," and his accuracy in business was, no doubt, the cause of his wealth and prosperity. Paheri not only filled every available space in his tomb with elaborate scenes neatly planned upon the walls, but when this important inscription, which was to provide for the future of his *ka* and carry down his name and virtues to posterity, had to be composed, he developed it to an unusual extent. It is unfortunate that it contains no scrap of biography, but this is a rare thing to find, and perhaps would have been considered in bad taste, excepting for a warrior.

In this inscription, as in most, there are expressions that are still obscure, and words that

---

¹ Pl. viii.-vi.
² The copies agree with the photograph in indicating ☾ incorrectly for △.
³ There is perhaps space for ⵇ in the break.

are quite unexplained. It would require much study and a long commentary to fully elucidate it, even where the meaning is certain. For the present we are satisfied to give the bare translation, since it displays many quaint ideas, and cannot fail to be interesting. The vignettes of the Book of the Dead would illustrate many passages in the first half of the inscription.

ll. 1-21. Prayers to the gods for the soul of Paheri, changing to benedictory addresses to Paheri himself in l. 4. *ll.* 22-35. Paheri speaking, reviews his own virtues. *ll.* 36 *to end.* Paheri's address to posterity, inviting them to recite prayers for him, and to read and imitate his virtues, and assuring them of the genuineness of the record.

1. May the king propitiate (?)
AMEN, lord of the thrones of the two lands, king of eternity, lord of everlasting, the prince possessing the great double plume, sole one in the presence, heir .... men and gods, living flame issuing from Nu (the watery firmament), light (?)   2. of mortals
NEKHEBT, the white one of Nekhen, lady of heaven, mistress of the two lands
OSIRIS, chief of the dwellers in the West (the Amentiu), lord of earth, the great one of the nome of This, mighty in Abydos
HATHOR, lady of the mountain, strong of heart amongst the gods
PTAH-SOKARIS, lord of the secret (tomb-) chamber
ANUBIS, lord of the Mouth of the Passage ....
[that they may give ghostly banquets: (the enjoyment of) offerings of provisions by the thousand; of gifts of flowers   3. and everything that grows upon the face (lit. " back ") of the earth by the thousand ; and of everything good and pure offered before the lord of eternity, by the thousand ; the receiving of food that has appeared in the Presence and milk that has appeared upon the altar; the drinking of waters that have been brought (?) from Elephantine; (and the breathing of) the north wind ....
[in the feast of .... the feast of the first day of the month), the feast of the month (2nd day), the feast of the 6th day, the feast of the half-month, the feast of the great appearing, the feast of the appearing of Sothis .... the greater and lesser heats, the first *mesper* (?) (3rd day) the birth of Isis, the appearing of Menu [1] (30th day of the month), the appearing of the *sem*-priest (4th day), the feast of service in the evening (5th day) and the feast of the inundation   4. the feasts of heaven in their times, and in that which belongs to the day for each day (i.e. the daily feasts)

1. *tu seten hetep*
Amen neb nesut tani, seten neḥeḥ, neb zet, áty neb shuti urti, ám [*baḥ?*] *ur, sensu .... reth neteru, teka ánkh per em Nu, shesep?*   2. *en homent*

Nekhebt hezt Nekhen, nebt pet, henut tani

Usir khent Amentiu, neb ta, ur Abez (?), *áa em Abṭu*

Het-ḥer nebt set usert áb emem neteru

Pteḥ Sekeri neb shetayt
Ánpu neb Re-setu
[*tesen per kheru......*] *kha em ḥetep zef, kha em ḥenket renpet*   3. *rețet nebt her sa ta; kha em khet nebt nefert nábt maát em baḥ neb neḥeḥ; shesep senu per em baḥ, ártet pert her utch; suri mu besqu em Abu; meḥy ....*

.... em ábțet, ...ent, ...ent, pert áat, pert septet, rekḥ áa, rekḥ nezes, mesper (?) *tepi, mest aset, pert Menu, pert sem, khet khaui, shesept áten*   4. *ḥeba nu pet er su-sen em kḥert ḥeru ent rá neb*

---

[1] Formerly read Khem.

and that there may be fitted upon thee sacred linen of fine stuff therefore, from the east-off vestments of the divine limbs: that thou mayest be sated (?) with pure oil: that thou mayest drink water upon the vessel (?) of the altar: that thou mayest partake of offerings therewith, attended by honoured persons,
(may all the above be granted) to the *ka* (ghost) of the prince of Nekheb, Paheri, justified.

5. O excellent satisfier of the heart of his master! mayest thou go in and out, thy heart enlarged, in the favours of the lord of gods; a good burial after a long life of honourable service: when old age comes and thou arrivest at thy place in the coffin and joinest the earth in the necropolis of the West, becoming a living soul. O! may it enjoy bread, water, and breath, may it make 6. its transformations into a heron, swallow, hawk, or egret, as thou desirest: mayest thou cross (the river) in the barge and not be driven back; and sail upon the waves of the stream; may thy life come to thee a second time; may thy soul not depart from thy body; may thy soul be strong with the glorious spirits, may the noble souls speak with thee, 7. thy image associated therewith receiving what is given upon earth; that thou mayest drink water, smell the breezes and enjoy thy heart's desire; may thy eyes be given thee to see, thy ears to hear speech: thy mouth speaking, thy feet walking, may thy hands and arms return to thee; may thy flesh be firm, thy muscles (?) pleasant, mayest thou rejoice in all thy limbs: 8. mayest thou reckon thy limbs entirely healthful, no ills in thee at all: thy stomach with thee in very truth, thy heart of former days: mayest thou go out to heaven and p[ierce the earth]............ .... may a summons be given thee daily to the altar of Unnefer: mayest thou receive cakes that have appeared in the Presence, offerings of the Lord of Ta-Zeser.

9. (all the above) for the *ka* of the prince of Nekheb (El Kâb), the prince of Anyt (Esneh): accountant of corn from Ant (Denderah) unto Nekheb, overseer watchful 10. and free of weariness, the scribe Paheri, justified.

Mayest thou eat the *shens*-cake with the god at the great staircase 11. of the lord of the divine cycle: mayest thou return from it to the place where he is amongst the chief divine officials: mayest thou walk with 12. them and associate with the followers of Horus: mayest thou depart and come without being turned back 13. or stopped at the gate of Tuat: may the doors of the horizon be opened to thee, and the bolts unlock themselves for thee; 14. and mayest thou arrive at the Hall of the two Truths, and the god who is in it salute thee, and mayest thou sit within the Amhet, and walk abroad in the City 15. of the Nile,

ârq-tu nek nâbu em peqt arini em se-feḳḥa ḥau neter: sasu-tu nek em zet nûbt: sura-ek uu her sa tep (?) kḥnu; sma-ek khet emem âri, sâḥ-ta em tepa ḥesgu

en ka en ḥā en Nekḥeb àu (?) Paheri maā-kheru

5. Mek âh men kḥ em m herf, äq-ek per-ek ab-ek fa, em ḥesut ent Neb neteru: qresṭ nefert em-kḥet aau ānukḥ: aant aisu, khenu-ek est-ek em neb ānkḥ, sma-ek ta em ḥert āmentet, kḥepar em ba ānkḥy: ḥeru sekḥem-s-f em ta mu nefu, urt-ef 6. Kḥeperu em beau ment em baḥ shenti pu mer-ek: za-ek m ākḥent uen ḥenḥen-ek; se-qetg-ek mit uug: kḥeper ān kḥ-ek em ahem-à; ān eui ba-ek er kḥet-ek; netri ba-ek ḥenā ānkḥu, meṭu-nek bau men kḥu, 7. senti-ek emem ari ḥer ghesep ṭeṭul ṭep ta; sekḥem-ek em mu, ṭepi-ek nefu, bâbā-ek em kḥert āb-ek; ṭeṭe-tu nek mert(?)-ki er maau, ānkḥui-ki er sezem zeṭut: er-ek ḥer metut, ret-ek ḥer ghemt, pekḥer-nek āui-ki, remen-ki; rut auf-ek, uefem met-ek, kḥent-ek em āt-ek nebt: 8. āp-ek ḥāu-ek ten azun, nen kḥut urt-ek rest; āb-ek mā-ek em uu muā, ḥāti-ek uek em ām ḥât: per-ek er pet uba-ek [ta(?)...............[u]āis-tu uek em kḥert ḥreu ḥer utḥu em Unen-nefer: ghesep-ek senu per em baḥ, fut-ā em neb Ta-Zeser

9. en ka en ḥā en Nekḥeb, ḥā en Ānyt, ḥeseb āt shau em Ant neferyt er Nekḥeb, kḥerp res tep 10. shu em ḥeḳi, ān Paheri, maā kḥeru

ām-ek ghens er ṭes neter er rut ur 11. en neb put neteru; uḥā-ek ām-ef er ba kḥer-ef em qab zazat tept: se-tutu-ek ememu 12. āri, kḥenemsu-ek ghemu Ḥeru: per-ek ha-ek, nen ḥenḥ-ek uen 13. ghenā-ek ḥer sba em tuat: un-tu nek āaui ān kḥet, seṣhen nek gert zes-14. seu; kḥenm-ek useḳkḥt ent maāti, uḥet-tu neter ām-es; ur-ek ḥems em kḥenn āmḥet, usten-ek em nut 15. ent Ḥāpi, fu āb-ek em seku-ek em ghet-ek en

and thy heart be enlarged with thy ploughing in thy portion of the Field of Aaru; mayest thou have possessions 16. of thy own getting, and may the harvest of fruits come to thee; may the rudder line be guided for thee in the barge, 17. and mayest thou voyage according to the bent of thy desire; mayest thou go forth every morning and betake thyself home (?) every 18. evening; may a lamp be lighted for thee at night-time until the light (of the sun) rises upon thy breast: may one say to thee 19. "Come, come into this thy house of the living!" mayest thou see Ra on the horizon of heaven and view 20. Amen at his rising: may thy waking be good each day, destroying utterly for thee all evil: mayest thou draw out eternity in pleasure of heart, 21. by the favour of the god who is in thee: thy heart (stomach) with thee not torturing thee, and thy food remaining in its place.

(all the above) to the ka of the scribe Paheri, justified: 22. he says

"I am a departed soul that was good to his lord, wise of countenance, without failure of heart: I walked 23. upon the road that I had planned, I knew that which results from life: I reckoned the boundaries in writing, 24. the dykes (?) with all the care (?) of royal affairs (?): all matters of the royal house L. P. H.¹ were like the Nile flowing to the Great Green (sea). 25. My mouth was firm in improvement for my master: I feared for the matter of the balance (of account): I did not forget (? or turn away my face), there were no exchanges, I did not. 26. receive bribes (?) from the results; my own [heart] guided me to the road of those who are praised of the 27. king: my pen made me very learned: [it] justified [my words before the] auditors (?); it caused 28. me to be distinguished (lit. "coloured"): I informed (?) the nobles..................
.... in the Presence: 29. my good quality advanced me .... 30. When I was placed upon the scales [I turned out true?], when I was counted (?) I had the full number.

31. "I prospered when I went out and when I returned, my heart was likewise: I did not speak to 32. deceive another: I knew the god who is in men, I recognized him: 33. I knew this from that: I performed matters according to the commands, I did not alter a message in delivering 34. it, I did not speak words above the station of serfs (?): I did not repent to those who had no 35. constant character. I brought (?) enjoyment (?) to the patient man—I who am praised and born of the body of the praised," 36. the prince

¹ Life, prosperity, and health ! a good wish that was generally uttered after naming the king; it is abbreviated in writing.

Sekhet Aaru; kheper khert-ek em 16. *art nek, int nek shemu em nahyt; aqa-tu nek aq em mákhent* 17. *sesq-ty-ek khed tet aberk; per-ek er ha teau tuau, un-ek tu teau* 18. *mesheen; seta-tu nek teka em kerh er uben shu her shenhet-ek; zet-tu nek* 19. *'aiui aiui em perek pen em ankhu,' tekyek rá em ánkhet en pet, se-kemh-ek* 20. *Amen ahen-ef: res-ek nefer em khert heru, ter-nek sep bu neb er tu, seb-ek uheh em nezem-ab* 21. *em hesut neter ámi-ek: áb-ek má-ek nen bethet-ef tu sefa-ek men er est áei*

en ka en án Paheri maá khera: 22. *zet-ef*

nuk sáh ankh en neb-ef, shesa her, shu em mehet-ab; shem-ná 23. *her uat nez-na si, rekh-ná peru en ankh: án heseb-ná teru em seshu, ufeha* 24. *em shesu neb en seten: khet nebt ent per seten, ánkh, uza, senb, má Hapi her seta er Uaz-ur.* 25. *Re-aí ruf her se-menkh en neb, sent kuá her khert zut: en sekhi her-aí, en tehu, en* 26. *shesep khesui em peru; sem-en ni [áb]-a zes-á er nut en hesyu en* 27. *seten, ár-en uí árí-á em rekh-khi,² sesmaá [-nef kheru-á em bah zaza ?]í: te-nef* 28. *áuu-aí; hub-aí seru a .... á em bah: se-ár* 29. *.en uá qeí-á nefer: nás k[uí k..................]yt* 30. *tet kuá her mekhat per-uá ...., áp kuí neh kuí*

31. *uza kuá shem-ná á-uá, áb-á kher máti: nen zet-á feru* 32. *er ky: rekh kuá neter ámi reth, sa-á su: 33. rekh-á pefa er pen: ár-na khet má ufetet, en sheb-á upt her semá* 34. *ses: en zet-á mefet ent bau meru: en shem-á en áutu* 35. *qet-sen: áunk án nekhu (?) en uah áb, hesy per em khet hesu,* 36. *há en Nekheb Paheri*

² Cf. pl. ii., l. 4.

of Nekheb, Paheri, justified, begotten of the nurse (tutor) of the king's son, the scribe Atefrura justified, and born of the mistress of the house 37. Kam, justified—he says

"Hear, ye who are to come into existence, I speak to you and there is no deceit 38. in what I say

"O ye living and existing nobles and people upon earth, servants of gods, and priests and those connected with them, every scribe who takes 39. the palette, skilful in divine words, and every excellent man of his inferiors, opening his mouth in boasting of 40. his occupation—May Ra, lord of Eternity, favour ye, and Nekhebt the white goddess of Nekhen; and all ye who are established in your (lit. his) offices, may ye bequeath them to your children

"41. if ye say 'May the king propitiate' in accordance with that which is in the writings, 'comings forth in answer to words' in the formula of the ancients like the utterance of a god, 42. and whosoever bends his hand in prayer may he act in the correct manner, and perform his devotion according to the rules, testifying 43. from the reading of the command here written: 'mayest thou have loaves by the thousand, beer by the thousand, and by the hundred thousand all things good and 44. sanctified by offering and pure'—to the ghost of Osiris, the prince of Nekheb and Anyt, who satisfied the heart of the superintendent of sealbearers 45. in the southward voyage (of inspection), the excellent scribe of accounts, Paheri, justified.

"I say to you and may cause you to know, that is by reading (this memorial), 46. it has no boasts (?), there is no injury or protest in it, 47. it is not a quarrel with another, nor a contradiction of a man who was miserable 48. in his time: they are pleasant words of cheerfulness, which the heart wearies not to hear: it is the breath 49. of the mouth which is not eaten, which hastens not and delays not: it will be well for you to do the like: [ye would have (?)] found [it true (?)] if 50. ye had (?) come here when I was in this land of the living, not a shame to my god. I have become a [soul] 51. well furnished, I have established my place in Kher-neter; my possessions of all kinds are with me, that I may not refrain from (?) answering.................. 52. my father('s mummy) was an object of reverent care to him whom he created, he lacked not (the son) whom he had begotten.

"May your hearing of this be pleasant."

The last sentence is the concluding formula in letters of the early period, and not inappropriately terminates the long address to visitors.

STATUES IN THE NICHE. Pl. ix.

Over Paheri's head is a vessel of water, symbolising purification (?), and his two great titles of "*ha*-prince of Nekheb" (El Kab, Eileithyiapolis) and "*ha*-prince of Anyt" (Esneh, Latopolis) are on either side, as well as the title of "scribe," which is repeated with each. Over the heads of the others is "his mother, whom he loves, the mistress of a house, Kem, deceased," and "his wife, whom he loves, the lady of a house, Henut-er-neheh" (*hemt-ef meryt-ef, nebt per Henut-er-neheh*): her name means "mistress for ever."

SIDES OF THE NICHE. Pl. x.

On the left wall of the shrine "the *ha*-prince, the superintendent of priests, the scribe" Paheri, and his wife, are seated before a table of offerings, while his son Amenmes performs a ceremony which enables the deceased to enjoy them—

árt tu hetep seten án sa-ef mer-ef Amen-mes: zet-ef 'sa-sen-ek nef en necht, khenem-ef em ántiu se-neter'

"Performing the ceremony of funerary offerings by his son, whom he loves, Amen-mes: he says, 'mayest thou breathe the breath of the north wind; may it smell of frankincense and incense.'"

Also, *en ka-ek, án udb*, "For thy ka, it is pure," words which were necessary for the acceptance of the funerary meal.

A little child, wearing the lock of youth, stands by the side of Henut-er-neheh. This may be one of the grand-children,[1] or perhaps the young prince Uazmes II.[2] Below the table is *sma khrt nebt nefert*, "partaking of all good things." Underneath the scene are six sons and daughters of Paheri, including Amenmes himself, seated on a mat, and smelling lotus flowers and buds.

On the right-hand wall of the shrine is Paheri himself offering to two royal children, and to his parents who had educated one of them. These are, on the first chair, *sa seten Uazmes*, "the king's son Uazmes," and *son-ef mer-ef sa seten Amenmes*, "his brother, whom he loves, the king's son Amenmes;" on the second, *menái en sa seten Uazmes Atefrura muâ khera*, "the tutor of the king's son Uazmes, Atefrura, deceased," and *nebt per Kem*, "the mistress of a house, Kem." Beneath the altar are the symbols of the objects offered—bread, beer, flesh, fowl, cord, linen, incense, ointment, gifts and flowers of all kinds, together with the sign for a thousand placed under most of them.

Below this scene are nine sons and daughters of Kem seated on the ground, including "her son who makes their name to live, the prince of Nekheb, Paheri" (*sa-es se-ânkh ren-sen*, &c.).

---

[1] See above, p. 18.   [2] See above, p. 6.

INDEX.

	PAGE
Aahmes, son of Aloua	5, 7, 8, 9, 21
Agriculture	12
Amenmes, son of Thothmes I.	6, 32
„ „ Paheri	9, 23, 24, 32
Animals	16
Ant (Denderah)	6, 29
Anubis	11, 21, 28
Anyt (Esneh)	6, 29
Apu, wife of Aahmes	5, 7, 8, 9, 21
Asses	16
Atefrura, father of Paheri	5, 8, 9, 21, 32
Attendants	12, 23
Baboon	28
Banquet	23–5
Belzoni	3
Boats	12, 15, 16, 21
Brugsch	4, 13
Buffoons	20, 22
Burton	3, 18
Butchers	26
Cattle, branding, 16; registering, 15.	
Champollion	3
Chariot	12, 13, 16
Corn harvest, 13; measuring, 15; ships, 15; sowing, 13; threshing, 14; winnowing, 15.	
Cortaz, M.	3
Denderah	6
Dog	24
Eileithyiapolis	6, 21
Eisenlohr, Prof.	7
El Kab	1, 6
Erman, Prof.	13
Esneh	6
Flax, combing, 14; harvest, 13; sowing (?), 13.	

	PAGE
Goats	16
Gold, receiving and weighing	16
Granary	15
Hathor	28
Hay	4, 18, 20
Hemuterncheh, wife of Paheri, 2, 8, 9; her relations, 18.	
Hieraconpolis	11
Human sacrifice	20, 21
Irby, Lieut.	3
Kam (Kem), wife of Atefrura	2, 5, 8, 9, 25
Kemhes	11
Khermeter	21
Latopolis	6
Lepsius	4
Lieblein	7
Mangles, Capt.	3
Maspero	13, 21
Mourners	19
Mummy, procession of	19
Musicians	25, 26
Nehebkau	18
Nekheb (El Kab)	1, 6
Nekhebt	1, 7, 27, 28
Nekhen (Hieraconpolis)	11
Net, making and using	17
New Year gifts	19
Nome	1, 6
Norden	3
Offerings	26
Osiris	11, 21, 28
Ostrich egg	18

FF

INDEX.

	PAGE		PAGE
Paheri, family of	8, 9, 18, 23, 24, 25	Stuart, Villiers	4
Paheri (brother)	5, 8, 23	Swine	16
Per-Hathor (Denderah)	6, 15		
Petrie	4, 7, 16, 18	Tentyra	6
Ploughing	13	Thothmes I.	6, 13
Ptah Socaris	28	„ III.	2, 3
Re-anti	10	Uazmes, son of Thothmes I.	5, 6, 9, 18, 32
Registration of cattle, 15; of corn, 15; of gold, 16; of offerings, 24.		„ „ Thothmes III. (?)	6, 18
Rekhmara, tomb of	19-22	Vineyard	17
Rosellini	3, 20	Vintage	17
		Virey, M.	19
Sacrifice, human, 20, 21; animal, 26.			
Spinning	17	Wilkinson, Sir Gardner	4
Statues	3, 32	Worship	10, 11, 25

CONTENTS OF PLATES.

Plate I. Façade and wall at side of entrance.
   II. Front wall, East half (the rest destroyed).
   III. West wall, south end : the official functions of Paheri.
   IV. West wall, centre : private life of Paheri.
   V. West wall, north end : funeral rites.
   VI. East wall, north end : a banquet, the principal group.
   VII. East wall, centre : a banquet, the ancestors and relatives.
   VIII. East wall, south end : worshipping the gods.
   IX. Back wall and statues in the niche.
   X. Sides of niche.

CORRIGENDA.

Pl. I. Scale in top left-hand corner: for 1 : 19 read 1 : 13.

Pl. V. Right-hand end of second row from top: the hair of the two dancing figures, of the four bearers of the shrine, and of the censer-bearer should all be plain, not frizzled. In the middle of the next row, the hair of the figure standing in the boat likewise should be plain. In the lower right-hand corner of the plate, the end of the crown of Osiris should be more nearly vertical, terminating in a knob.

Pl. VII. The body-line of Hepu should be completed between the arms.

PLATE I.

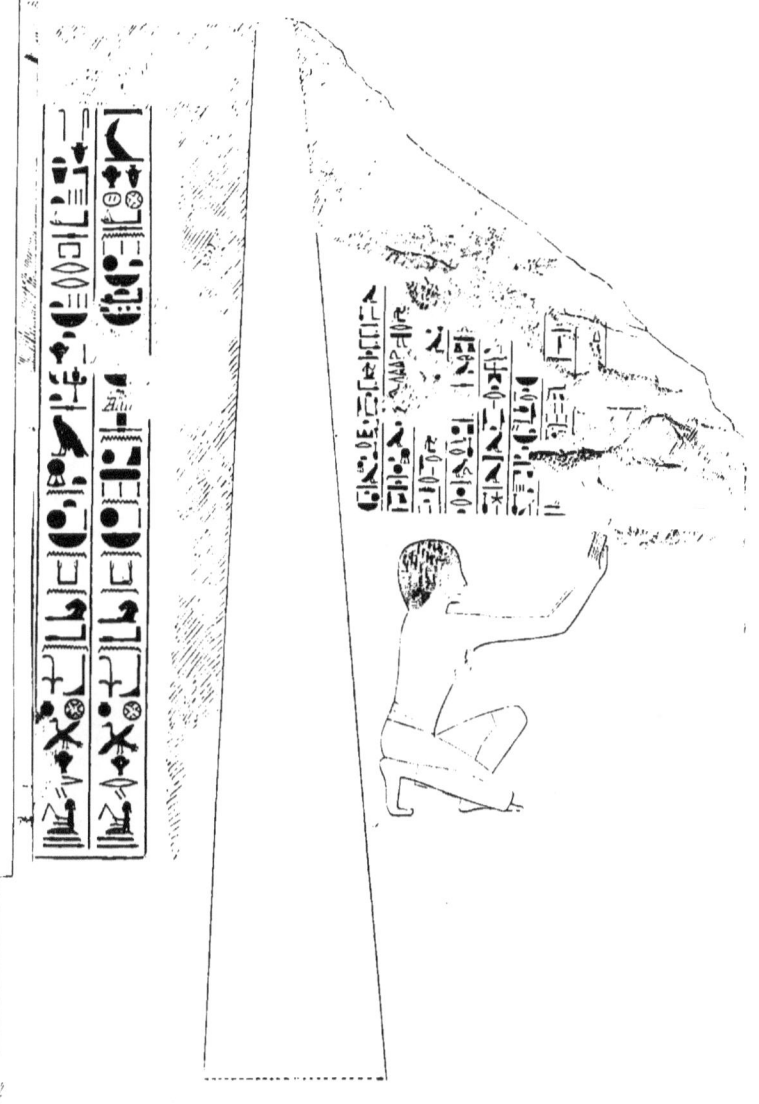

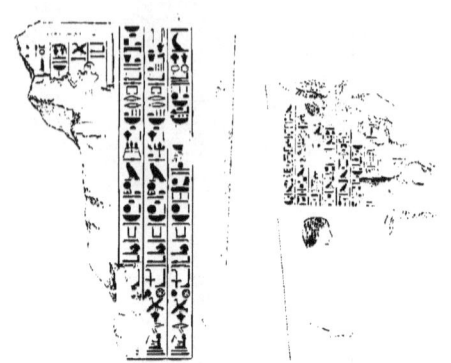

TOMB OF PAHERI. PLATE II.

PLATE III.

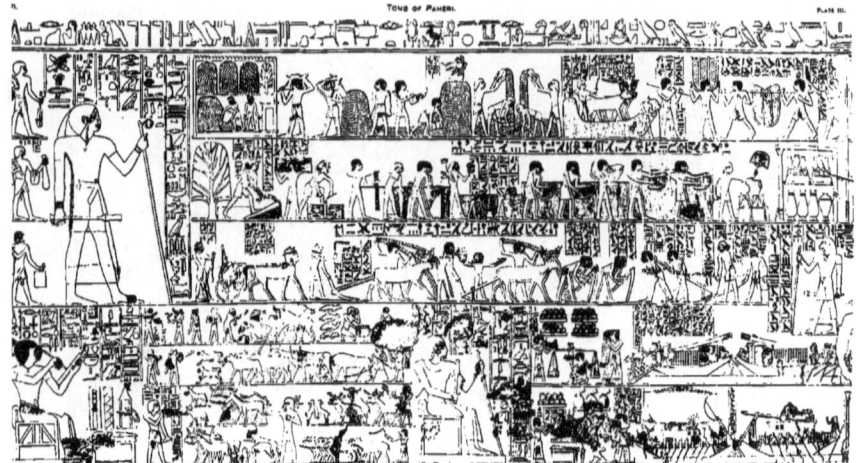

1:71.

WEST WALL, CE

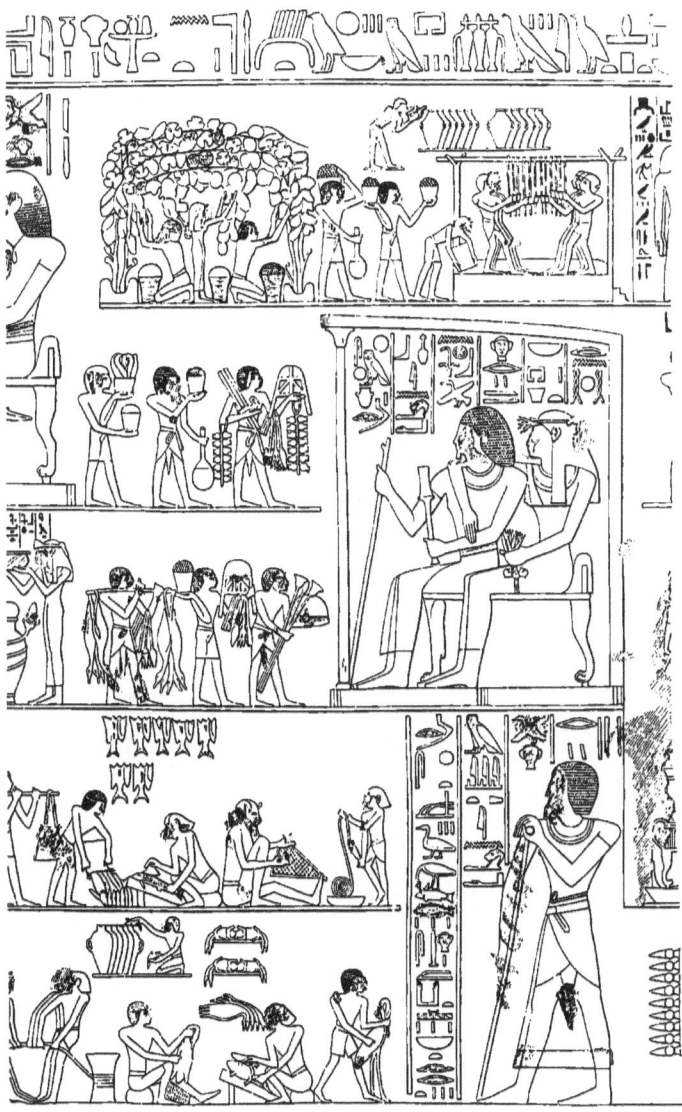

RE: PRIVATE LIFE OF PAHERI.

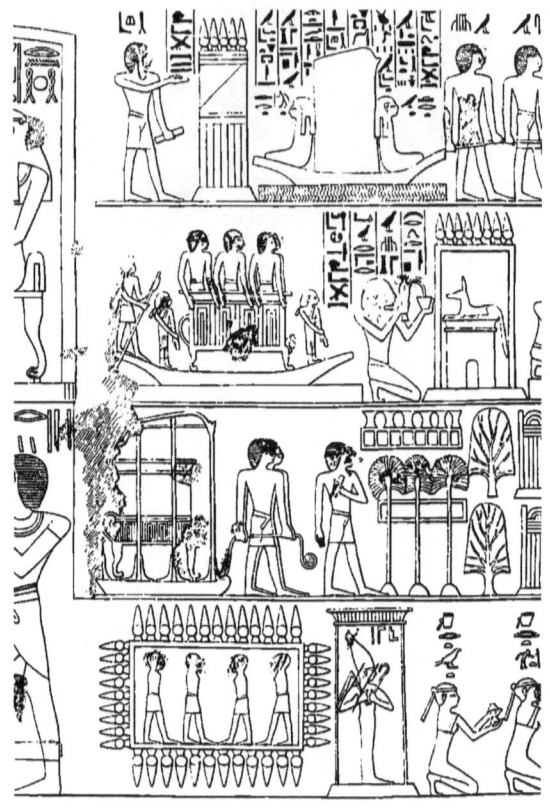

WEST WALL.

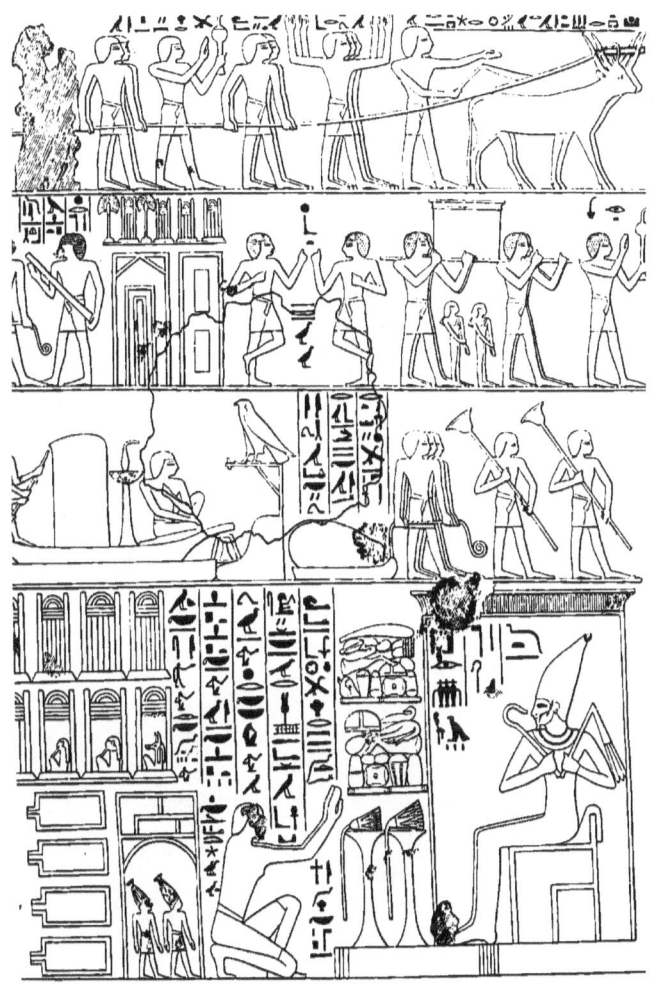

'H END: FUNERAL RITES.

EAST WALL, NORTH END:

BANQUET, THE PRINCIPAL GROUP.

1:71.

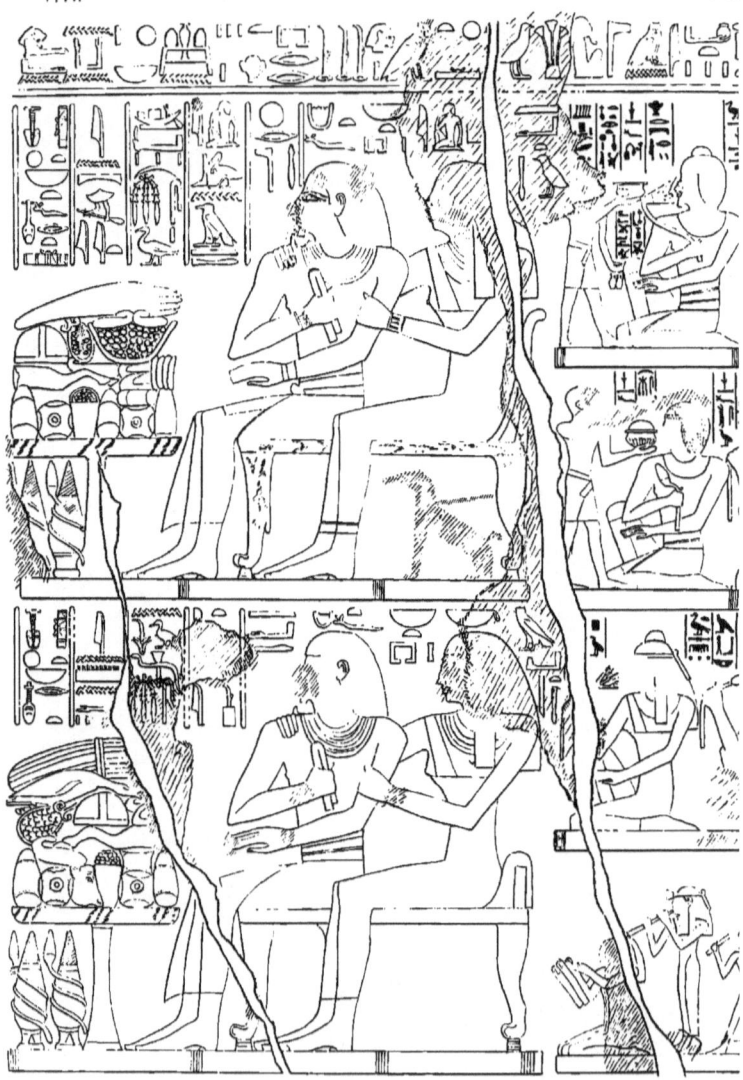

EAST WALL, CENTRE: A BANQU

THE ANCESTORS AND RELATIVES.

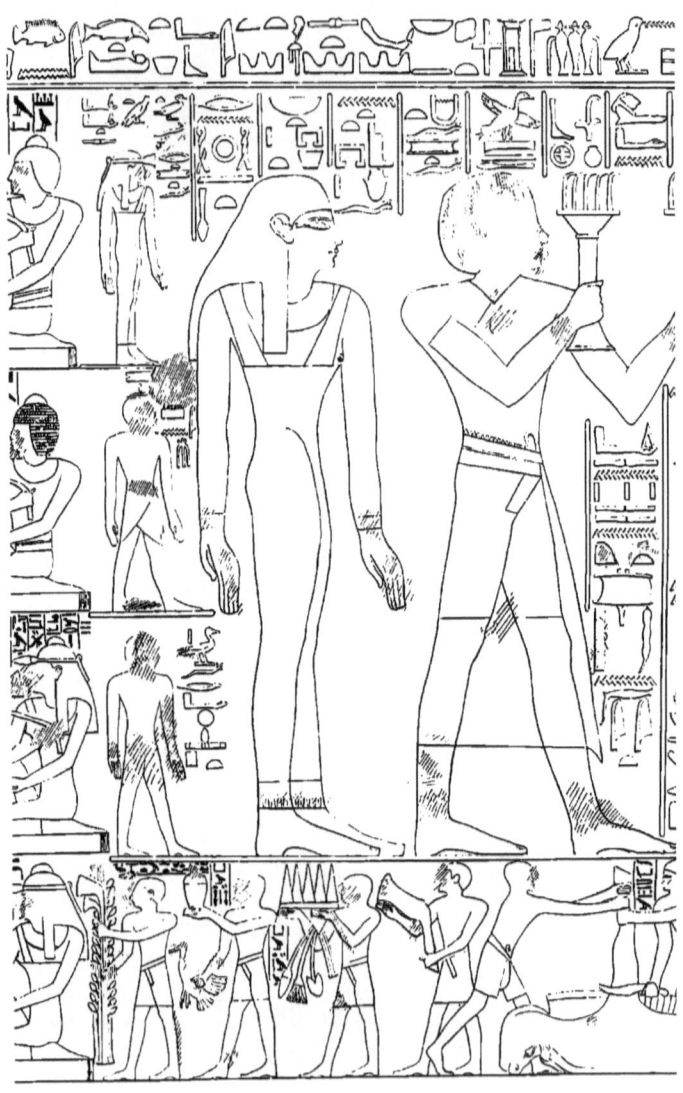

EAST WALL, SOUTH

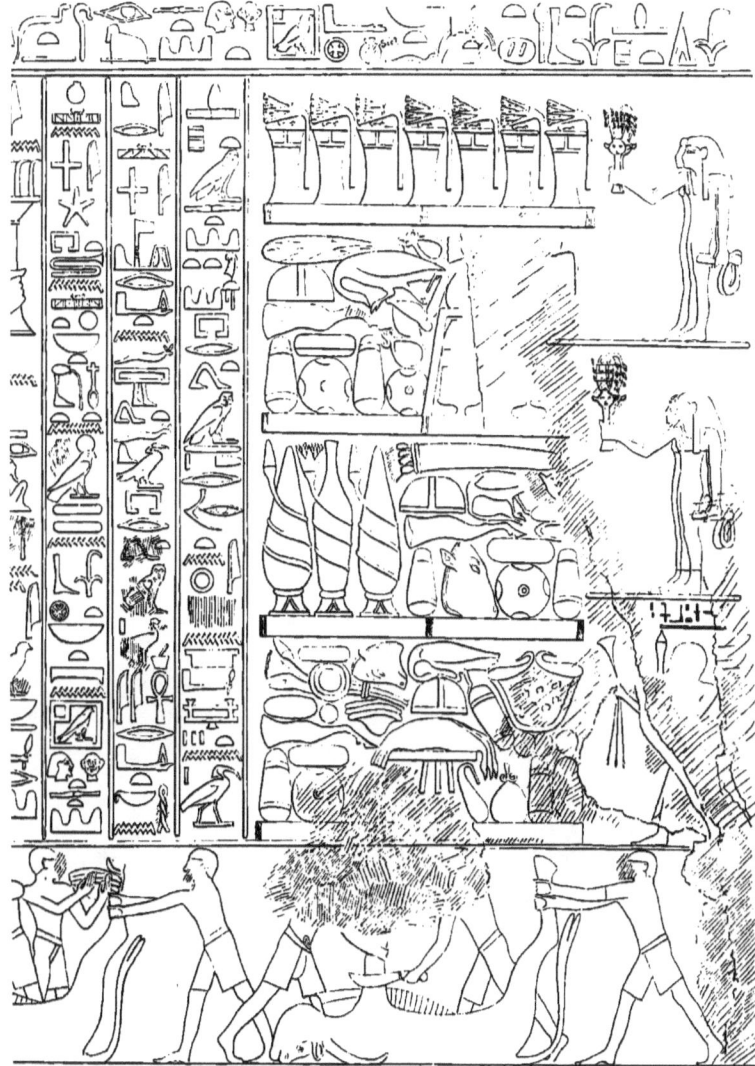

WORSHIPPING THE GODS.

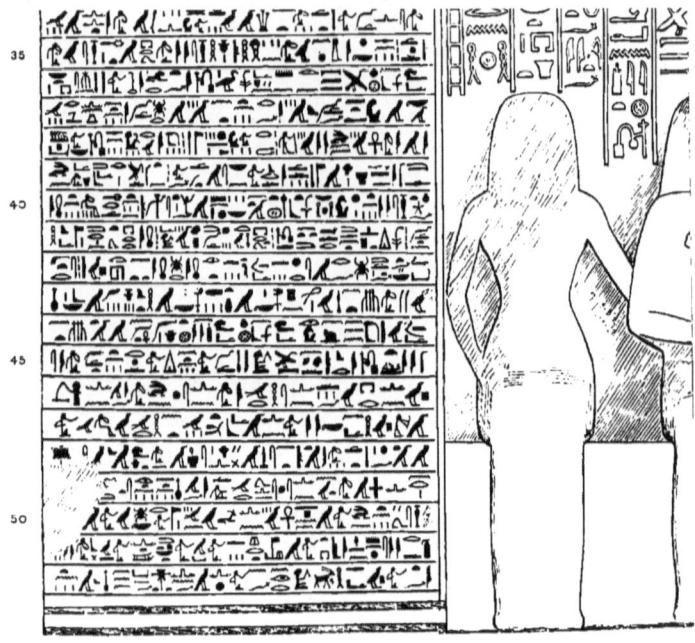

BACK WALL, AND

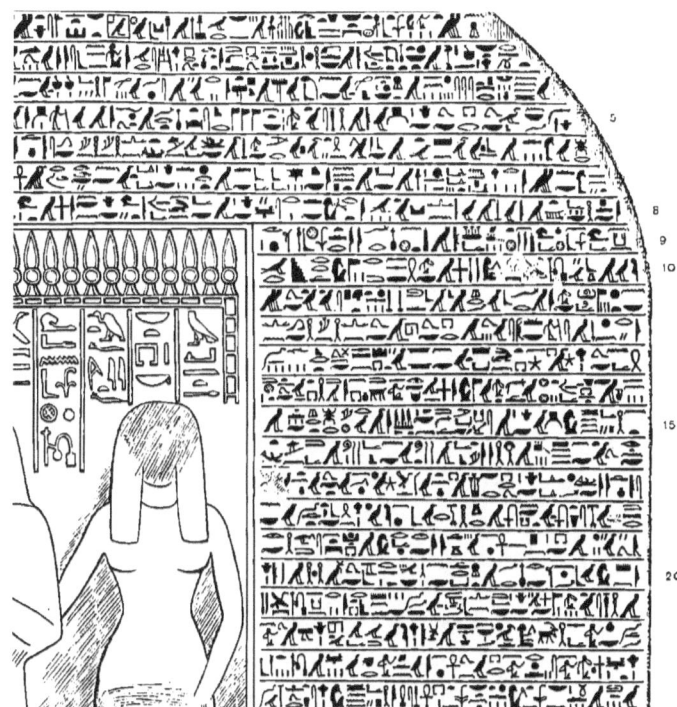

TOMB OF PAHERI.

WEST SIDE.

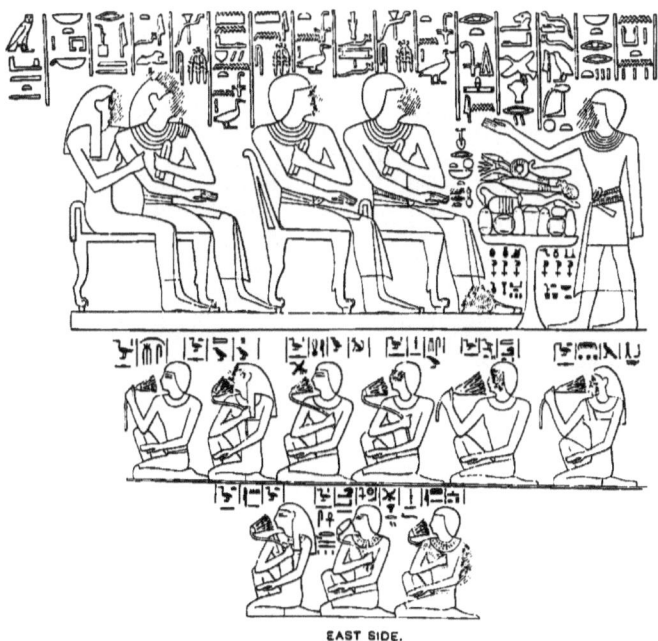

EAST SIDE.

SIDES OF NICHE.

EGYPT EXPLORATION FUND PUBLICATIONS.

I. *Th. Store-City of Pithom and the Route of the Exodus.* Memoir for 1883-4. By EDOUARD NAVILLE. With Thirteen Plates and Two Maps. Third Edition. 1888. 25/

II. *Tanis.* Part I. Memoir for 1884-5. By W. M. FLINDERS PETRIE. With six-teen Plates and Plans. Second Edition. 1888. 25/

III. *Naukratis.* Part I. Memoir for 1885-6. By W. M. FLINDERS PETRIE. With Chapters by CECIL SMITH, ERNEST A. GARDNER, and BARCLAY V. HEAD. With Forty-four Plates and Seven Plans. Second Edition. 1888. 25/

IV. *Goshen, and the Shrine of Saft-el-Henneh.* Memoir for 1886-7. By EDOUARD NAVILLE. With Eleven Plates and Plans. Second Edition. 1888. 25/

V. Part II., *Nebesheh (Am),* and *Defenneh (Ta'panes).* Memoir for 1887-8. By W. M. FLINDERS PETRIE. With Chapters by A. S. MURRAY and F. LL. GRIFFITH. With Fifty-one Plates and Plans. 1888. 25/

VI. *Naukratis.* Part II. Memoir for 1888-9. By ERNEST A. GARDNER. With an Appendix by F. LL. GRIFFITH. With Twenty-four Plates and Plans. 1889. 25/

VII. *The City of Onias, and the Mound of the Jew, the Antiquities of Tell el Yahûdîyeh.* Extra Volume for 1888-9. By EDOUARD NAVILLE and F. LL. GRIFFITH. With Twenty-six Plates and Plans. 1890. 25/

VIII. *Bubastis.* Memoir for 1889-90. By EDOUARD NAVILLE. With Fifty-four Plates and Plans. 25/

IX. *The Hieroglyphic Papyri from Tanis.* An Extra Volume. Translated by F. LL. GRIFFITH and W. M. FLINDERS PETRIE. With Remarks by Professor HEINRICH BRUGSCH. With Fifteen Plates. 1889. 5/

X. *The Festival Hall of Osorkon II. in the Great Temple of Bubastis.* Memoir for 1890-1. By EDOUARD NAVILLE. With Thirty-nine Plates. 1891. 25/

XI. *Ahnas El Medineh.* Memoir for 1891-2. By EDOUARD NAVILLE; and *The Tomb of Paheri at El Kab.* By J. J. TYLOR and F. LL. GRIFFITH. 1894. 25/

SPECIAL EXTRA REPORTS.

The Season's Work at Ahnas and Beni Hasan. By EDOUARD NAVILLE, PERCY E. NEWBERRY, and G. WILLOUGHBY FRASER. 1891. 2s. 6d.

Archæological Report, 1892-3. Edited by F. LL. GRIFFITH. With Seven Illustrations and Maps. 1893. 2s. 6d.

PUBLICATIONS OF THE ARCHÆOLOGICAL SURVEY OF EGYPT.

Edited by F. LL. GRIFFITH, B.A., F.S.A.

First Memoir (to Subscribers 1890-91). *Beni Hasan.* Part I. By PERCY E. NEWBERRY. With Plans and Measurements of the Tombs by G. W. FRASER. Forty-nine Plates. Price 25s.; to Subscribers, 20s.

Second Memoir (to Subscribers 1891-92). *Beni Hasan.* Part II. By PERCY E. NEWBERRY. With Appendix, Plans and Measurements by G. W. Fraser. Thirty-six Plates. Price 25s.; to Subscribers, 20s.

IN PREPARATION

Third Memoir (to Subscribers 1892-93). *El Bersheh.* By PERCY E. NEWBERRY. With Forty-eight Photo-lithographic Plates, and Two Coloured Plates. Price 25s.; to Subscribers, 20s.

Hon. Vice-President for America:
CHARLES DUDLEY WARNER, ESQ., L.H.D., LL.D.

Vice-President and Hon. Treasurer for America:
REV. W. C. WINSLOW, Ph.D., D.C.L., LL.D., &c., Boston, Mass.

www.ingramcontent.com/pod-product-compliance
Lightning Source LLC
Chambersburg PA
CBHW030254170426
43202CB00009B/743